ALSO BY LYNNE COX

Swimming in the Sink

Elizabeth, Queen of the Seas

Open Water Swimming Manual

South with the Sun

Grayson

Swimming to Antarctica

TALES *of* AL

TALES *of* AL
The Water Rescue Dog

THE MAKING OF A SUPER ATHLETE

Lynne Cox

6/02/22

To Delena,
Hope you enjoy the
happy ending!
All my best,
Lynne Cox

ALFRED A. KNOPF ~ NEW YORK ~ 2022

THIS IS A BORZOI BOOK
PUBLISHED BY ALFRED A. KNOPF

Copyright © 2022 by Lynne Cox

All rights reserved. Published in the United States by Alfred A. Knopf,
a division of Penguin Random House LLC, New York, and distributed
in Canada by Penguin Random House Canada Limited, Toronto.

www.aaknopf.com

Knopf, Borzoi Books, and the colophon
are registered trademarks of Penguin Random House LLC.

Library of Congress Cataloging-in-Publication Data
Names: Cox, Lynne, [date] author.
Title: Tales of Al : the water rescue dog / Lynne Cox.
Description: First edition. | New York : Alfred A. Knopf, 2022.
Identifiers: LCCN 2021038997 (print) | LCCN 2021038998 (ebook) |
ISBN 9780593319376 (hardcover) | ISBN 9780593319383 (ebook) |
Subjects: LCSH: Water rescue dogs—Anecdotes. |
Human-animal relationships. | Water rescue dogs—Training.
Classification: LCC SF428.55 .C69 2022 (print) | LCC SF428.55 (ebook) |
DDC 636.7/0886—dc23/eng/20211001
LC record available at https://lccn.loc.gov/2021038997
LC ebook record available at https://lccn.loc.gov/2021038998

Jacket photographs: Donatella Pasquale; (inset) Barry Lewis / Alamy
Jacket design by Jenny Carrow

Manufactured in the United States of America
First Edition

For Steven

Because of the dog's joyfulness, our own
is increased. It is no small gift.

—MARY OLIVER, *Dog Songs*

Contents

TALES *of* AL

1

Hot Chocolate and Beth

The hot summer sun set, the humidity was high, and the mosquitoes and black flies were humming as the moon rose above the slowly swaying pine trees along the edge of Snow Pond in Maine. It was time to escape from the heat and weight of the world and go swimming.

I jogged from the family camp across the soft lawn in my swimsuit with sweat sliding down the backs of my knees, hair sticking to my head, swatting mosquitoes, and breathing in black flies. I dove off the wooden dock into the water.

A cool breeze as soft as a whisper flowed over my body and suddenly my hands cracked the surface of the inky black pond. Water exploded around me and I felt myself gliding deeper and deeper into the blackness. My body was absorbed by the darkness and sounds above the water were extinguished. It was so peaceful. I only heard my heart beating and my breath rising in a slow stream of silvery bubbles. My body was suddenly light. I felt like I was floating in a dream. I was seven years old and in a state of awe.

There was something magical and thrilling about being in the pond at night when the colors of the world disappeared and the water and land became shades of black, white, gray, and sparkling silver. Shapes, lines, textures, and light became more abstract; it was like stepping into a black-and-white photograph. In the darkness I could merge with the water and the world and feel a deeper connection to both.

My arms were outstretched, giving me balance, and my feet were dangling below. I sensed something moving around my feet, fanning the water and moving close. Suddenly I felt it nibbling on my little toe. I jumped, screamed, and kicked my feet as whatever it was started sucking harder, and I tried to pull my toe from its mouth. And then I felt a swarm of creatures nibbling all of my toes. Fraught with fear, I frantically pulled to the surface, sprinted to the dock, curled my legs under my body, and held on to the side where my mom and dad were standing.

"Something is biting my toes!" I yelled.

My mom laughed in her warm musical voice and said

the same thing happened to her when she was little. They were sunfish, small fish the size of her hand. They ate whatever they could fit in their mouths. She said there were larger fish: white and yellow perch, bass, pickerel, and eels that lived in the lake grass and near the lily pads, but they were not interested in eating toes. That made me relax, but not for long.

Elizabeth, our three-month-old Dalmatian, whom we called Beth, was standing near the dock's edge making sorrowful sounds. Her whimpers and whines were piercing the quiet night. In the darkness the 332 black spots all over her white body were difficult so see. A glimmer of moonlight reflected in her soft brown eyes, and she looked afraid. She was panting. Her breath was hot on my face. I petted her to try to reassure her, but she would not be consoled. She knew we were going swimming and did not want to be left alone. She pulled away and protested with loud and anxious barks. She tucked her tail between her hind legs and crouched down. She wanted to be with her family.

My mom jumped in the water and turned toward shore. When Beth saw her dark form moving, she went wild and ran to the end of the dock. My mom scooped Beth up in her arms and carefully held her in the water. Beth started moving her tiny paws in a beginner's dog paddle, making a lot of splash.

My mom guided Beth toward my dad, and when she

was right in front of him, she let Beth go. He immediately caught Beth, praised her, and lifted her up to give her a hug. She surprised him by licking him all over his face. He laughed hard, a deep belly laugh, and for a few moments, he held Beth and waited for her to catch her breath. My mom took a few steps back, and then my dad gently set Beth down in the water so she could paddle to my mother. They made sure that Beth felt safe and she could trust them. My parents were teaching Beth to swim the same way they taught my brother, sisters, and me.

My siblings joined us in the lake and we swam with Beth. She wanted to keep going and going, but my mom said she had done enough for the evening. Beth was a little puppy and this was a new exercise for her. My mom did not want her to overdo it or she would be sore and overtired and not enjoy swimming.

Before my mom lifted the puppy from the water I asked if I could hold her for a minute and feel her swim. Mom made sure I had a firm grip on her, and Beth started paddling at a good pace. I felt her speed and power, until Beth suddenly froze.

A high, haunting, and beautiful sound burst through the air. The sound became suspended in the sky and echoed across the pond. The darkness made it feel eerie.

My dad whispered, "It's a loon, a large black water bird with red eyes and a pointed beak." He explained that loons are amazing swimmers and divers and they build their nests in sheltered coves or on the islands near the center of Snow Pond—places undisturbed by people. They choose areas where the water is clear where they can see below the surface. In the shallows they can hunt for salamanders and frogs, and they can hold their breath for fifteen minutes and dive up to fifty meters underwater to catch small fish. Their feet are large and they use them like flippers.

The loon was calling his mate. He hooted.

A few moments later, with a long wavering call, she answered.

He replied. He was close to us, his voice louder than hers. He called again, homing in on her plea, trying to find their nest.

She directed him with a long, mournful wail.

Their calls and answers started to overlap, and the pine, beech, and maple trees rimming the shore created a natural amphitheater, amplifying the cascading birdsong.

We saw a flash of silver and heard a large splash. Beth jumped. She was startled but not afraid. The loon surfaced only ten meters away. Moonlight reflected off his silvery feather necklace and made it glow and flicker as he paddled cautiously past us.

The female continued calling with long, loud wails. Her mate answered and suddenly flapped his wings hard and fast and lifted his heavy body off the rippled pond. She continued making her haunting calls and hoots until they united in their nest.

My dad explained that loons were special to the Algonquin Indians, who believed that the birds carried divine messages. The Algonquins were right. We can see the mystery, wonder, and magic in the natural world through loons and their exquisite songs.

Beth was starting to get chilled. She was shivering in my hands. My mom took her from me and carried her out of the water. My dad gently dried her with a towel. Beth loved the feeling of the towel brushing against her skin. And when he dropped his face near hers, she stuck her wet black nose onto his cheek. He laughed and carefully dried her ears, making sure there was no water remaining in the canals.

When my dad set Beth down, she wiggled and wiped her body against his long leg, wagged her whiplike tail, and then she sprinted across the lawn and ran in a large circle around us. We were a swimming family and she seemed to love swimming as much as we did.

The night had become chilly, so we hurried into the camp, where my grandparents were waiting. We crowded around the black iron woodstove and felt the warmth radiate across our bodies. Our muscles eased and relaxed. The burning wood smelled so good; the smoky fragrance of sweet maple, earthy oak, and spicy pine filled the kitchen.

My grandfather Arthur asked us to step back so he could lift a burner off the stovetop and feed more wood to the fire, so my grandmother Elaine could heat some milk and make us hot chocolate. Inside the stove, the wood glowed bright orange and yellow and crackled. Sparks flew as my grandfather added split logs to the hole in the top and the room gradually became warmer. A few minutes later, my grandfather handed me a cup of steamy hot chocolate. Carefully, I took it with both hands and drank it. The chocolate was sweet, creamy, and rich. The drink tasted delicious and warmed me up after the cool evening swim.

Dog-tired, Beth curled up on a soft rug made by my grandmother. It was a braided rug, and I loved it. I asked her how long she spent working on it and she said three years. That seemed forever to me. She assured me that three years was not a long time, and that as I got older the years would fly by, but time was always precious. She hugged me—I think to make sure I would remember that moment. She was warm and soft and smelled delicate, like lilies of the valley.

"You work on things you love. That makes you happy and helps you bring beauty into the world," she said.

Finishing my hot chocolate, I studied the rug carefully. Grandma Elaine used wool fabric strands of turquoise, bright blue, forest green, heather gray, soft orange, and butter yellow. She braided them with her gentle hands in beautiful patterns, and shaped the braids into a large oval. The colors and patterns she created in the rug made it a work of art. I liked to lie on it and look at the different color combinations and feel the soft braids.

My grandmother glanced at Beth. I thought she would

say something about a wet dog lying on her beautiful rug. She did not like dogs, having been bitten by a cocker spaniel when she was a child. They still terrified her. She never walked near a dog, and if one got close to her, she ran away. My mom had also been bitten by a cocker spaniel when she was a child. Sometimes fear travels through generations and stays. But my mom did not accept a fear of dogs. She discovered she should not pet a sleeping dog, realizing that it startled them, and she never did it again. She now loved dogs.

I got down on the floor and sat on the braided rug with Beth near the warmth and light of the woodstove. She placed her head in my lap so I could rub her velvety black ears and read to her and to myself. She loved mysteries and I did too. It was probably the way I read to her; she liked hearing the clues and wanted to know where the bones were buried. When I talked to her, she seemed to know that I was discussing the clues. She looked like she was considering what I told her.

She let me rest my head on her back.

Sometimes Beth rolled over and I petted her soft pink belly while reading to her. When she fell asleep, her eyes twitched beneath closed lids, her black nostrils flared, and her breathing quickened, and she whimpered. Her spotted legs extended above her body and contracted as she ran through the air and dog-paddled in her dreams.

Beth would stay with me as long as I was reading.

When I carried my book upstairs to bed, she would snuggle in beside me and we would read until the lights went out and then I would turn on my flashlight. We would read together into the wee hours of the night when the world was peaceful and words were more magical. I could imagine new things about life and Beth would move onto the pillow and we would be cheek to cheek. There was nothing quite as wonderful as reading a good book beside a good dog.

It was not long before Beth was swimming with us in the pond. She loved being in the water. If she saw the family in the pond, she would tear down the lawn, run across the dock, and leap in with a huge splash. She would swim to each of us and herd us together, but she was more focused on my mom. Maybe it was because she knew my mom filled her food bowl. But I think it was something deeper. They had a special connection.

They loved each other. It was easy to see it in the way they looked into each other's eyes, the way Beth prodded my mom with her nose and wagged her tail to get her attention, and the way my mom stroked Beth's head with adoration. Beth watched over my mom. She was happiest in her company. When my mom went grocery shopping Beth hopped in the red Buick station wagon, sat in the passenger's seat, and stuck her head out the window with ears flapping and intense brown eyes watching for anything that might pose a danger.

Toward the day's end, when my mom took a break and stood by her easel to work on her oil paintings, Beth lay down near her feet. The room filled with the spicy smell of turpentine and the sounds of Beth's long and steady breathing and of my mom's palette knife as she scraped short and rapid strokes around the canvas. Often, she paused to check her progress and petted Beth to reassure her that all was well. When my mom finished painting for the day, Beth's coat would be speckled with cadmium blue, red, yellow ocher, sap green, Payne's gray, and colors my mom blended on her palette.

Beth was always vigilant when my mom was in the water. My mom floated vertically with her arms extended as naturally as a water lily. She was at home in the water. Her breaststroke was easy, with powerful pulls and kicks and long glides. Her backstroke was smooth and her head was relaxed and her freestyle was graceful and efficient. Only small flashes of white water rose from her hands as they entered the water and her pull was strong and steady, her glide was long, and her flutter kick was just enough to keep her balanced in the water. Beth did not understand that my mom was okay. She would sprint along the dock and leap into the pond, circling her and trying to grab my mom's wrist in her mouth to pull her toward shore. My mom would say, "No, Beth," and gently push her away, but Beth was determined. She would chase my mom, but my mom would swim away from her fast. Maybe this was something in Beth's genes. Dalmatians are bred to be firehouse dogs, to lead horses and firemen to fires, and protect them. That instinct was strong inside Beth and she felt she needed to protect my mom.

Our family swims in Snow Pond with Beth became one of my favorite things. I also loved to eat black raspberry ice cream with her. I got the top of the cone and she got the crunchy bottom.

Part of my love for swimming came from Beth. My parents encouraged my connection with Beth because I liked to wander and explore and they thought that having our dog with me would make it safer. My mom and dad let me give Beth her middle name. Giving a life a name filled me with a sense of responsibility and awe and it made me feel like I was growing up. I spent months considering what to name her.

Holding her spotted wiggly body in my hands, feeling her tiny heartbeat, her warmth, the softness of her fur, her ears, and her body, and seeing the brightness in her eyes, I knew there was something miraculous about this little puppy. I tried to think of a name that would describe her spirit. She was like a purple crocus blossom that emerged from an island of ice after a long, frigid New England winter. She was strong and vital, but also delicate and exquisite.

"What do you think of Elizabeth Crocus Cox?" I asked her.

Beth did not react. "Crocus" did not sound right. I wondered if there was another word for it. Searching through dictionaries and thesauruses, I couldn't find anything. Finally I created a name and tried it on her.

"Do you like the name Snow Flower?" I asked.

Beth wagged her tail fast, jumped up, put her paws on my shoulders, and licked across my face. By naming her, I felt a stronger connection to her.

I trained Beth to lie near my feet under the table during supper, and at the end of the meal I snuck her treats. She ate whatever I gave her without jiggling the tags on her collar or making a sound.

My mom served the family liver once a month because my parents believed the high iron content of the filter organ was good for us. Attempting to disguise the strong flavor, my mom sautéed bacon and onion in a heavy cast-iron frying pan to add sweetness and smokiness to the liver. She served it with the onion and bacon on top with a side of mashed potatoes. The texture of the liver was spongy, and its flavor infused the bacon and onions so everything tasted chalky and metallic. I was told I had to eat it, but I couldn't.

Beth always saved me. She placed her head in my lap and devoured the liver piece by piece and nudged me with her wet nose, requesting more.

We were best friends. Exploring the woods, splashing in streams, wandering through fields of high grasses, catching bugs, eating wild blueberries, and watching gray squirrels were some of the best things we did during the day. And at night when hot, humid air collided with cold air, storms often rolled over Snow Pond and thunder shook the camp so much that my grandfather said that people were bowling in heaven. Sitting on the floor beside Beth, I wrapped my arm around her back and we listened to the rumbling and crashing thunder and watched the brilliant blue flashes of lightning zigzagging across the inky black sky.

Pouring rain streamed down windows, blurring the view of the lawn, trees, and pond. Roaring wind buffeted the camp; waves shattered across the pond. We were immersed in the storm, and Beth was a brave dog. None of this bothered her. It was exciting for her. We sat together feeling the energy being unleashed around us.

In the morning after a storm, when the pond was capped with a thin silvery layer of cool water and the air was light, sweet, and fresh, Beth dog-paddled beside me, her head even with mine. We raced between the dock and shore, swam around my grandparents' property to neighboring camps and farther up the pond to watch frogs on lily pads catching bugs. It was fun and because of her, I fell in love with swimming and with dogs.

That was why many decades later, I was transfixed by what I saw on my computer screen.

2

Flying Dogs

Sitting at home at my desk, I was watching a video on my computer unlike anything I had ever seen.

Beneath the hazy blue Italian Alps on a strip of green grass beside the aqua waters of Lake Iseo, a long line of dogs on leashes waited restlessly beside their owners. There were soft-coated golden retrievers, enormous Newfoundland dogs, athletic yellow, chocolate, and black Labradors, sturdy spaniels, and alert German shepherds.

The dogs started barking wildly when they saw a black Newfoundland wearing a bright red swim vest break from the line, pulling two men with her. One man was wearing a red full-length wet suit and the other was in dark shorts and a T-shirt. They were holding a handle on top of the

Newfoundland's harness and steering her toward a wide patch of grass. Despite her size and heavy body, she was light-footed and running quickly, and she sprinted when she saw a helicopter circling overhead.

The yellow and red helicopter began its descent. The air was filled with the roaring, thumping, and whining of the helicopter's rotors, overpowering all other sound.

As the helicopter touched down, two people in red wet suits climbed out of the passenger compartment and stood on a wide metal step. They crouched down, leaned forward as if they were preparing to jump out.

Gusts of wind from the rotors smacked the dog's face, tossed dirt into the air, and blew her fur back. The deafening noise from the helicopter was painfully loud, but the Newfoundland was not deterred. She was completely focused. She ran in step with her escorts and knew exactly what to do.

Two meters from the helicopter, she leaped into the air. Her escorts lifted and hoisted her toward the helicopter door and the two people on the helicopter step caught the handle on her harness and strained to lift her on board.

Immediately she moved into position. She turned around in the passenger area and stood on guard between the two people in wet suits. One of the crew spoke into a radio giving the all-clear signal.

As the helicopter lifted off, the Newfoundland leaned out the door and watched the land drop rapidly below her. Quickly, people and dogs became black dots on the small green rectangle.

I shifted in my chair, curious about what they were doing and where they were going.

As the helicopter climbed higher into the sky, the dog's mouth was opening and closing. She was tasting the air. Her nostrils were moving in and out quickly. She was smelling the air for clues as she was hunting with her crew.

I was focused on the dog. Amazed. Fascinated. Intrigued. I had never seen a Newfoundland jump into a helicopter. I did not think they were that light-footed and agile and I had never seen a Newfoundland fly. I could not understand why this dog was not afraid. Most dogs are terrified of loud noises. They cower, hide, or run away. But this wind-battered Newfoundland was not concerned. It looked like she loved to fly.

The helicopter climbed quickly into the blue sky spotted with puffy white clouds and banked over the deep dark waters of Lake Iseo. The pilot flew over a large white rescue boat and turned along the shoreline. The Newfoundland dog and crew continuously scanned the craggy shore and water below.

Small fishing boats plying through the rippled water dotted the lake. A few sailboats drifted slowly across the water in the warm breeze. Ferries cruised to and from the large islands below. In the hazy distance small villages built in the Middle Ages clung to hillsides and spread out along the lake's shore. Soft white, pastel-yellow, saffron, orange, ocher, and cream-colored buildings reflected in the lake in wavering pools of color like an Italian impressionist painting.

Something was moving below. The Newfoundland spotted it first and signaled the crew with a deep bark and a tug on the harness. A man about two hundred meters from shore was splashing wildly. It looked like he was struggling to keep his head above water.

The pilot lowered the helicopter. The dog looked at her human partners to make sure they were ready. While still high in the air, the dog leaned out of the door. The crew adjusted their grip on the dog's harness and held her tightly. She leaned farther, pulling them almost out the door. Barking and stomping her front paws, she alerted them that there was someone in the water in distress.

The crew restrained her so she would not jump too soon, but she continued to lean forward. It did not matter that the helicopter was too high off the water; she was prepared to leap.

When the helicopter was about three meters above the surface her owner jumped in and the crew launched the dog. The Newfoundland flew through the air, dropped rapidly into the water, hit the surface hard, and disappeared.

A few seconds later, she popped up in the rotor wash. Stinging spray hit her in the eyes and face, but she had a position fix on the man in the water. Somehow, she paddled quickly to her owner and they swam to the victim through large waves created by the whirling helicopter blades.

The dog swam beside the man, turned, and offered her harness. He held on to the handle, and with the owner supporting him, the Newfoundland pulled them both four hundred meters to shore.

When they touched the sand, the struggling man stood up, smiled, and thanked the dog. They climbed from the water onto the beach. The owner took the dog's head in his hands and praised her for a job well done. They were both grinning.

I had never seen a dog leap from a helicopter into a lake. I had never seen a dog rescue a struggling person in the water. I had never seen a dog that courageous. I had never seen anything so unusual. It was like watching an astronaut walk on Mars. I was amazed by what I saw on my computer screen. It was difficult for me to comprehend what I had witnessed. Dogs are afraid of heights. People are too. I remember how scared I was when I was thirteen years old and climbed to the top of the ten-meter platform at the Belmont Plaza Pool in Long Beach, California.

I had to climb so many steps to the top of the tower that I had to stop three times to catch my breath. And when I walked to the edge of the platform and looked all the way down to the water, I could not believe how high up I was. The fifty-meter pool looked small and I could barely see the black lines painted on the bottom, five meters below the surface. I wondered what it would be like to fall that far. I wondered how fast I would fall. I wondered how bad it would feel if I did not hit the water straight on, if I did something wrong and landed on my back. I wondered how far I would go underwater and if I would have enough air to make it back to the surface. I stood on the edge of the ten-meter platform not realizing that I was holding my breath until I started to feel dizzy. Then I told myself I had to be calm. I had to breathe.

I looked down around the diving area. No one was in the water below me. It was safe to jump. I looked across the pool where my teammates were doing a kicking series. They were watching me. I was stalling, trying to find some courage.

The more I looked, the farther down the water appeared to be. It was awful. I thought maybe I could turn around. I could climb down the steps. The ten-meter jump was not something I had to do.

But there were so many steps to get back down to the ground and I thought they might be slippery. I might fall and get hurt. I returned to the edge of the platform. Hands sweating. Heart beating hard and fast. I told myself I could do it. It was just a simple jump. Nothing to it. All I had to do was take one big step.

It was nothing like what Olympic divers do every day. I watched them train. What they did was mind-boggling. The Olympic divers did triple somersaults, back handstands, twists, and pikes. They were strong, quick, agile, graceful, and courageous.

I had to remind myself that they did not start out that way. I had watched them when they were just learning how to do their dives. They learned parts of their dives and rehearsed them on the pool deck before they climbed to the ten-meter platform. Then they would practice the motions of each dive one more time before they jumped off.

When they attempted a new dive, they sometimes didn't get enough push off the platform. When that happened, they didn't rotate quickly enough doing a somersault, or they got into a pike position and held their ankles too long, or they lost concentration and did not do what they needed to at the right moment. They landed wrong.

Sometimes they hit the water so hard that the bang, thud, and splash echoed through the natatorium. The coaches and other divers would move quickly to the edge of the pool to make sure the diver surfaced. Sometimes they hit so hard and it hurt so much that they needed to stay underwater and compose themselves before they would surface and swim slowly to the side of the diving pool. Shaken, they climbed out of the water like an old person. Their bodies were bright red. Somehow their coach would talk them through their mistake and help them correct it and rehearse the move on the pool deck. Then they would attempt the dive again. Sometimes they wiped out two or three times before they made the dive or the coach decided it was time to attempt a different one. Occasionally divers were injured. I remember seeing a woman spin out of control. She hit her ear so hard the impact punctured her eardrum. Blood was pouring out of her ear when she climbed from the water. She had to wait a few months before it healed, and then she returned to the platform and nailed the dive. It took lots of courage to be a diver.

I could not imagine doing a somersault off the platform. I could barely imagine jumping. But Phyllis, my swimming friend, shouted to me from across the pool: "Come on, Lynne. Just jump!"

She had done it and said it was scary. So I gathered my courage and took one big step.

I fell fast. I was counting; one thousand one, one thousand two, one thousand three, and I teetered to one side. It felt like I was falling forever. I tried to straighten out, fell backward, and hit my back so hard I heard it smack the water. The whomp must have echoed across the pool.

My back stung worse than a horrible sunburn. The pain brought tears to my eyes. I continued traveling down through the water. I had to push off the bottom hard to crawl to get to the surface before I ran out of air. I swam to the side of the pool and held on to the gutter. My swimming friends were watching me. I waved to signal I was okay. But my back still throbbed in pain.

Replaying the rescue video on my computer, I wondered how a dog could do such an unnatural thing. Not only did the Newfoundland jump from a great height, she had to leap from a moving helicopter. She was a large dog and she hit the water hard. It exploded around her. She must have felt the sting of it. She dropped below the surface and had to hold her breath. I wondered how she did it without getting water up her nose. It all looked so simple, but that happens when one prepares perfectly, when one is ready physically and mentally for the task at hand. Still, I wondered if this Newfoundland dog had been born with this courage or if she learned how to be brave.

Courage is something that is revealed when one is faced by adversity. It may originate from somewhere in the heart, and often we find courage by working through fear. I've always wondered if the ability to be courageous is something that is born within us, something that emerges at the moment we need it, or if it is what we learn through taking on life's challenges. That dog was courageous and I had to find out more about her.

Looking at the video a third time and stopping it here and there, I watched for the dog's hesitation. Was this something she wanted to do or was she being forced to do it? I realized that she did not hesitate once. She was eager to participate and the people with her were trained and serious. I wrote down the name of the group that was doing this: Scuola Italiana Cani Salvataggio—Italian School of Rescue Dogs. I did more research and discovered that they worked with the Italian Coast Guard—Guardia Costiera.

I had to learn more. I wondered where the dogs come from, where they were trained, how they learned to be fearless. Was this fun for them? What happened to the dogs that didn't want to leap? Were they forced to participate? Were they pushed out of the helicopter? I wondered if the school was legitimate and if the dogs really helped rescue people from the water. I contacted John Shaulis, a friend who had been a naval aviator stationed in the Mediterranean, to see if he knew more.

John mentioned that he had been involved in joint military exercises with the Italian Navy. He loved dogs and flying and Italy, so I asked him if he had heard of the water rescue dog school. He had not, but he was as intrigued as I was, and through a military attaché, he put me in touch with a friend who knew someone at the United States embassy in Rome. She in turn contacted the Guardia Costiera and spoke with Admiral Angrisano, who worked closely with Ferruccio Pilenga, the founder and president of the school. He and his school colleagues provided invaluable support to the Guardia Costiera. The men and women and their dogs served as volunteer life-guards and helped the Guardia patrol Italian lakes and seas. They made Italian waterways safer for boaters, swimmers, kayakers, and people who enjoyed being in, on, and around the water.

Admiral Angrisano told me the water rescue dogs were known throughout Italy and around the globe for their lifeguarding service. They often interceded before people got into trouble and they saved many lives each year. The dogs had recently been invited to travel to Germany and Switzerland to train and do lifeguard work on lakes and seas there.

He put me in touch with Donatella Pasquale, the vice president of the school who had owned Alyssha, a famous lifeguard dog.

Immediately I sent Donatella an email and asked if I could visit her school, to see how they trained their dogs and how they worked with the Guardia Costiera.

The next morning, I received her invitation to come to northern Italy. Thrilled, I could not wait to go.

3

By Design

Donatella met me at the Milan airport and offered to take one of my carry-on bags. She was a petite and strong middle-aged woman wearing a khaki top and pants. Her hair was short and dark brown. Her eyes were filled with excitement. Smiling at me, she said she was happy I made it to Italy. Quickly we walked from the airport terminal to the parking lot. Al, her female Newfoundland dog, was waiting for us in the car. Donatella did not like to leave Al for very long.

When Al heard Donatella's voice, the Mazda MPV where she was waiting for us started swaying. To move the vehicle that much she had to be big. Donatella said Al was exceptionally strong and could pull three to four times her own weight.

Al started barking.

Speaking in a steady voice, Donatella tried to calm her as she lifted the rear door and opened the largest dog crate I had ever seen.

Al sprang from the vehicle. She was huge—larger than a year-old bear cub. Landing on the ground, she danced around Donatella and jumped up, trying to swipe her huge pink tongue across Donatella's face.

Donatella ducked, turned away, and spoke tersely to her. But she was too happy, overjoyed to see Donatella. She was her world. Her fun. Her life. She gave her food for energy, food for thought, food for treats. Al loved to be with Donatella. Al just loved everything about her and was trying to demonstrate that in every way. Wagging her tail rapidly from hip to hip, she nearly knocked Donatella over.

Donatella insisted that Al sit. Finally, she obeyed and Donatella managed to clip a leash to her harness.

I had never seen a Newfoundland as exuberant as Al. And I had never seen one that looked like Al. The Newfoundlands I knew had long, thick black coats or long black-and-white coats. Al was different. By comparison she was exotic. She had a long brown fur coat that fell softly around her like a giant cape. Other Newfoundlands had large beautiful brown eyes, but Al's eyes were gold and bright and filled with intelligence: exquisite and intriguing.

Al saw that I was studying her. She tilted her head

down, raised her inner eyebrows, and looked up at me, giving me puppy eyes. Slowly she sashayed her hips and furry tail and invited me to touch her.

"Is it okay if I pet Al?" I asked.

"Please do, she loves people," Donatella said, holding the leash tightly but allowing Al to stand.

I approached Al slowly so she would remain calm and scratched her behind her soft ears. She groaned softly and rested her bear-sized head against my hip. I felt her double coat. The outer layer was long and wavy and composed of long, coarse guard hairs that served as a barrier that repelled water, caught dirt and debris, and kept Al's undercoat and skin dry. Her undercoat was downy and as soft as a kitten's fur. It was shorter, denser, and fluffier than the outer coat, keeping Al warm in cold, wet weather and cool in hot, humid weather.

Like all Newfoundlands, Al lost fur daily. When people petted her, wispy strands sailed through the air, stuck to fingers, flew into faces, attached to clothes, and spiraled onto furniture and the floor. It was dog confetti—a celebration of the dog. Spring and fall were a fur fest for Newfoundlands.

The change in sunlight affected the dogs' circadian rhythm and caused them to blow coat—shed handfuls of fur for up to a month. They shed heaviest in spring, losing their old heavy winter undercoats, and in autumn they shed their lighter summer coats.

When Al would blow coat Donatella brushed her and

swept up her fur daily. Normally Donatella brushed her three times a week, blow-dried her once a week, and bathed her every ten days, but in summer when she was swimming more often, Donatella sent her to the groomer at least once a week. Al resigned herself to being brushed. She rested on one side and then on the other while Donatella removed loose fur and untangled her coat.

Brushing Al was essential to her health. If her fur became matted her skin would not be able to breathe and moisture would be trapped between her undercoat and skin, creating hot spots and skin problems. Donatella also checked for mats around Al's ears where water could be trapped and cause ear infections. She trimmed the mats to allow more airflow to dry out the ear canals and prevent infection. Donatella also had to keep the hair between Al's toes trimmed to prevent burrs being caught in her fur and burrowing into her skin.

Caring for her Newfoundland was time-consuming, but Donatella wanted her to be happy and healthy, and Al basked in the attention Donatella gave her. It also helped strengthen the special bond between them.

Donatella said that Al had always been a self-confident girl with little or no fear and no phobias. She had a strong character and it had been relatively easy to teach her something, but Donatella worked constantly with her in five-minute sessions throughout the day to accommodate Al's short attention span. And she had to train her to be less exuberant and to modulate her excitement toward people. She wanted to meet and greet everyone without thinking that maybe she could scare someone or induce unwanted reactions.

Donatella said that she never needed to be tough on Al; she needed to be consistent with her. When Al did what Donatella asked, Donatella rewarded her with her full attention. If Al did something wrong, Donatella didn't scream at her or hit her; she would take Al by the scruff of her neck and move the skin from side to side, then bring her back to where the unwanted behavior began and tell her she was an "ugly dog." And Al understood that she had done something that Donatella didn't want her to do.

Donatella said the most fundamental and important part of her relationship with Al was to have Al choose to be with her above all else. This behavior was not natural; it had to be learned. Donatella said this was the key to understanding what kind of relationship she had with Al and how strong the relationship was between any dog and owner. Donatella tested Al to see if they were building a relationship. She encouraged her to jump into the water and play with other people and dogs. She would wait until Al was engrossed in the activity and then she would slip into the water without a sound. If Al noticed her, stopped playing, and raced to Donatella's side, Donatella knew that she would always have her attention and that they were building a strong relationship.

When Donatella tested Al, sometimes the dog noticed her, but often she continued playing. Donatella was disappointed. She knew she had to keep working with Al, and it was not easy to train her.

Donatella explained that Newfoundlands are not more difficult to train than other breeds; they are different because they have their own timing. If you give an order to a German shepherd, he immediately executes it. If you give a retriever a command, the dog can't wait to respond. If you give a direction to a border collie, before you finish speaking the border collie has already completed the task. A Newfoundland hears your order, knows perfectly what you want, thinks if he or she wants to carry it out and if that's what you want him or her to do, then he or she does it. This completely changes in the water, where the Newfoundland transforms itself from a big and clumsy land animal to an agile and impetuous swimmer.

Rubbing my hand along Al's long, wide back, I felt the firmness of her broad shoulders and taut muscles. Al let her jaw drop open. She surprised me with a sloppy wet kiss. I laughed with delight.

"She is incorrigible," Donatella said, shaking her head. She was not amused by Al's antics. "Do you need a cloth to wipe your face?"

"I don't mind," I said.

Donatella explained that we were going to Lake Idroscalo to meet Ferruccio Pilenga and some other members of the school.

Al heard Donatella say the word "go" in Italian and immediately jumped into the back of the vehicle. Donatella secured her in her crate. I opened the door on the passenger side and noticed black paint on the vehicle's white hood. It was an enormous portrait of a Newfoundland.

Donatella smiled and said that she got the idea for the image and had it professionally painted. She was serious about her dogs and fully committed to the school.

We drove through the streets of Milan, an industrial city, financial hub, and global center for fashion and design. I caught glimpses of store windows that displayed elegant dresses, fine men's jackets, rich textiles, sophisticated leather shoes and handbags, elegant silk scarves, and ties by world-famous Italian designers: Prada, Versace, Armani, Marta Ferri, and Ferragamo,

As we wound our way through the busy streets of Milan, we were surrounded by beautiful and aerodynamic cars designed in Milan. There were Fiats and Alfa Romeos, a green Maserati, a white Lamborghini, and a bright red Ferrari. Italian drivers liked to test the limits of their cars and themselves. They drove fast, close, and creatively—finding spaces between vehicles where at first glance none existed. Cars came so close that I closed my eyes. But Donatella was totally focused on her driving. She was alert and anticipated the movement of vehicles around her, swerving, stopping, or speeding up whenever she needed. She could not allow for a moment's lapse in focus. Driving through Milan was an adrenaline rush.

I held on to the door handle so hard my hand turned white. I held my breath three or four times, as if holding my breath and sucking in my sides would help us fit between the cars pinching us from all directions.

City noise, congestion, construction zones became a blur. Looking away, in the distance I noticed the elegant spires of the Duomo di Milano and I realized that Milan had been a center for new ideas for a long time. It was a city that supported creativity, a place where people used their imaginations and discovered new ideas. It was a place that valued human expression. So, it made a lot of sense to me that the idea of creating a school for water rescue dogs was welcomed and embraced in Milan.

We turned a corner and entered an entirely different world. Donatella slowed the car and rolled down the window. Warm air flowed through the car. I took a deep breath and smelled fresh mowed grass, sweet water, and dust, finally relaxing as we entered an enormous park.

We drove near the soothing blue waters of Lake Idroscalo, the music of the water lapping the shore. A breeze swirled around the trees and gently rustled the leaves, creating a hush broken only by the song of Italian sparrows and the caw of crows.

Driving slower and speaking softly, Donatella explained that the lake was man-made. It was opened in 1930 as a seaplane airport, and when people stopped using seaplanes for transportation the lake was transformed into a park. She laughed and said the lake was also known as the Sea of Milan, but it was a tiny sea. It was only about 3 kilometers long and 250 to 400 meters wide. Swimming, kayaking, canoeing, rowing, paddling dragon boats, sailing, and waterskiing were popular sports there. The city fathers reserved a special place on the lake for the Scuola Italiana Cani Salvataggio. Its location was highlighted on the map of Lake Idroscalo.

Donatella parked the vehicle beside a row of ancient pine trees and we climbed from the car. Ferruccio was waiting for us by the lake.

"Come and meet," she invited.

We walked down a gradual slope to the edge of the lake.

As Donatella introduced me to Ferruccio and his dog Mas, Al reared up and hugged Ferruccio and jumped up to greet Mas.

Demanding that Al sit and behave, Donatella spoke to her firmly. She did not seem to understand. Donatella had to repeat herself three times. Finally, Al sat.

Ferruccio said something to Donatella in a sympathetic tone.

Donatella nodded but was visibly frustrated, explaining to me that she needed to leave us while she and Al went to work with some students, waiting on the beach about two hundred meters away.

4

Chicken Sandwich and an Entrée

Ferruccio shook my hand, smiled, and glanced at the lake. He had a suntanned face, short, styled white hair, and a neatly trimmed beard and moustache. It was clear he was a waterman. As he looked at the lake with reverence, respect, and excitement, his brown eyes were focused on the water. He had been studying it, watching it move, seeing the wind pattern change from dark blue in the center of the lake where the wind was stronger to light blue near shore where the water was sheltered from the breeze. He was checking it again; he knew the water was always changing. I think he was deciding where it would be safe to swim. I was evaluating the conditions too. That was my nature and the reason I had been able to break the world record for swimming the English Channel when I was fifteen years old, be the first woman to swim across Cook Strait, and be the first person to swim the Strait of Magellan, around the Cape of Good Hope, across the Bering Strait, in Antarctica, and to achieve sixty channel swims.

But I never jumped into any water without first researching it and then deciding whether it was safe to enter. From local experts, I learned that each waterway was unique and in constant flux, and for those reasons it was exciting to attempt a channel swim.

From Reg Brickell, one of the best English Channel pilots, I learned about tides, currents, and water movement through channels, how to judge a ship's speed and whether a swimmer could swim fast enough or alter course to avoid being run over by a tanker. The Chilean Navy and Chilean pilots taught me about the strong tidal changes in the Strait of Magellan and how the tides create rips and whirlpools that can sink ships. They showed me how to read the changing sea and how to avoid areas where whirlpools were forming. From fishermen and a special forces team in South Africa, I learned about huge waves that were generated in Antarctica by calving glaciers and how to read a set of incoming enormous waves. California surfers showed me how to enter and clear wave impact zones quickly to avoid being tumbled and crushed. Inuit living on Little Diomede Island and a helicopter pilot flying between mainland Alaska and the island explained unstable weather in the Bering Strait and how fast wind can move into a region and transform the water's surface from calm sea to a raging ocean. Frogmen showed me how to sight underwater hazards and assess risk. Sailors explained how to see the changes in the color of the water's surface to read the shifting direction of the wind. In Antarctica I learned from the Quark Expeditions crew how to track the speed of icebergs and how to avoid swimming into them. Lifeguards and health departments informed me about water quality, and shark experts and marine biologists taught me about sea animals that I needed to avoid and those that would swim with me safely.

I was curious about the man who had been inspired to create the school and who devoted his life to people and dogs and making sure they were safe in the water.

I wished I could speak Italian or he could understand more English. I wanted to tell him that I love being in the water, that it gives me a sense of freedom, and that while I swim ideas flow around in my head like water itself. Through the tug of the tides, I feel the pull of the moon. Through the spin of the earth, I feel the currents. Sometimes I flow with the tides and currents and sometimes I swim against them, but that makes me stronger.

"You learned to swim when you were a child?" I asked.

"Yes. And I always loved dogs," he responded.

"Me too. I think we are *simpatico*," I said.

Ferruccio was wearing a red wet suit and life vest on his compact body. Mas sat beside him and was also wearing a flotation vest.

They were the man and dog I had seen in the video on my computer. I had flown one quarter of the way around the world to meet them and I was thrilled to be with them, excited that they were going to show me their world.

Mas looked at the water the way Ferruccio did. She had the same connection to it.

"Ah, Mas, you are beautiful—*bellissima cane*," I said in my limited Italian, stroking her head. She felt like a teddy bear.

Mas wagged her tail. It thumped softly in the sand. She understood my American Italian. She looked at me and studied me the way Al did. I saw the gentleness and goodness in her brown eyes.

Ferruccio was a sensitive man who read the expressions of people and dogs easily. He could see that Mas and I immediately liked each other. He explained that he needed to make sure that I was not afraid of Mas. She was a big dog and sometimes people were afraid of big dogs.

I told him that I loved dogs and I had been around big dogs all my life, but that I respected them and was careful with them. A dog wagging its tail might mean it was friendly or it might signal that the dog is nervous or scared or feels threatened so it might bite.

That was what Ferruccio needed to hear. He needed to know that he could trust me around the dogs and that I would listen to him. He needed to know that I would not put any us of in harm's way.

Ferruccio loosened his grip on Mas's leash and let her sniff my hand. She wagged her tail so fast that her entire body wiggled. She probably smelled the chicken sandwich I had for lunch. Ferruccio was watching Mas to see what she thought of me.

A friend called this evaluation process the "sniff test." He said dogs openly did this to one another. They sniffed other dogs and through their sensitive noses and brains were able to smell their intentions. In a whiff, they could determine if another dog was friend or foe. People did the sniff test more subtly by observing and questioning one another.

I smiled and thought of my dad. He told me that dogs could often read people better than people could. He said if I was going to date someone, he wanted our family dog to meet the man first. If the dog disliked him, the man was not worth dating. The family dog was always right.

Somehow Mas had signaled to Ferruccio that I was okay because his face relaxed.

He told Mas to sit and gave her a hand signal. She was so well trained she obeyed immediately.

Dogs constantly watch people. They read their facial expressions and can interpret them. Mas watched Ferruccio to read him and know what he wanted her to do. Mas knew that she could depend on Ferruccio and she was devoted to him.

Ferruccio petted her gently behind the ears, looking at her with love. He had owned Mas since she was a puppy and had trained her right from the beginning. He had had other Newfoundlands, but Mas was immediately responsive and became special.

I asked if it was true that Italian people were known for speaking with their hands to clarify or emphasize what they were saying. A friend told me that I did that all the time; she once held my hands and I had difficulty speaking.

Ferruccio laughed and said it was true Italians were known for using hand gestures a lot. He used them in communicating with dogs and with human students so they would better understand him. Also, if they were a distance away, they could often see what he was saying with his hands better than they could hear him. When he pointed in a certain direction dogs could interpret that gesture and know where to look or where to go.

He pointed at a dog in the distance. Mas immediately turned her head to see what he was pointing at and then looked expectantly at Ferruccio. As he petted her ears, she relaxed and looked up at him with adoration.

Speaking in a warm, affectionate voice, and in a mixture of English and Italian, he said Mas was smart and had great intuition. She was gentle and careful with puppies and children and people and dogs. Consistent and hardworking, she was always ready to swim the extra kilometer.

I think I understood most of what he said. But the tone Ferruccio used when he spoke about Mas reminded me of my favorite swim coach. It occurred to me that Ferruccio was also a coach of dogs and people.

One of the trainers, Roberto, a large, tall man, joined us to help translate, which made better communication possible. He explained that Mas was one of the world's greatest canine water rescue dogs. She particularly enjoyed teaching other dogs how to become rescue dogs.

"Dogs teach other dogs?" I asked.

Ferruccio nodded.

"Dogs may come from different countries and understand the different languages that people speak, but dogs all bark in the same language," I said.

"Dogs are remarkable beings," Roberto echoed.

He continued to explain that their sense of smell was 10,000 to 100,000 times more acute than a human's sense of smell. They could use their noses to locate people on land and in the water too.

I thought scent was diluted by water and dogs therefore lost the scent. But I learned about a black Labrador retriever in Seattle that could smell floating orca scat in the Puget Sound up to two kilometers from shore. And an

English springer spaniel named Barra that lives in Scotland, a member of a K-9 search and rescue team, who can detect the scent of a body in a river, firth, or lake. The scent of the body's gasses rises to the surface of the water and Barra can pick up that scent. Alexandra Horowitz, a world-renowned researcher on dog cognition, explained how acute a dog's sense of smell is. She wrote that a person might be able to notice a teaspoon of sugar in a cup of coffee, but a dog could smell a teaspoon of sugar in an Olympic-sized swimming pool.

I wondered if dogs could smell peoples' emotions, because a human's body chemistry changes with their mood shifts. Maybe that happens with dogs too. Maybe dogs could smell other dogs' emotions.

I told Ferruccio about my yellow Labrador named Cody, who would sit beside me when I had coffee on Main Street in Seal Beach. People would stop by and say hello to Cody. One day, K. A. Colorado, an artist, came by and sat beside me. Cody got a good sniff of him as he passed, and Cody stood up, walked around me, and sat beside K.A., a man we just met. Cody always sat beside me, but he leaned on K.A. and let him pet him. K.A. told me that his dog had just died. Cody knew that and was comforting K.A.

Another time Cody and I were sitting on a bench in Seal Beach. A young boy in a wheelchair and his father passed by. Cody walked over to the boy and sat beside him and let him pet him. The boy's father said they just lost their assistance dog. He knew that Cody was sitting beside his son to comfort him. Ferruccio observed that Cody was responding to the scent of their emotions.

Ferruccio had an easy way about him. He listened well and was open to ideas. He craved learning and that was probably why he had so many people and their dogs wanting to attend his school.

But I was curious. I had read about all sorts of obedience schools for dogs, watched dog trials on television, and loved Lassie, the smartest and sweetest collie I had ever seen. But his idea to start a school for water rescue dogs was so creative and unusual.

5

Terranova—Newfoundland

Long ago Ferruccio heard a story about an ancient sailing boat. The ship with 150 sailors was caught in a terrifying storm. The wooden ship was being pummeled by gigantic waves and it felt like they would crack the vessel in half. Terrified by horrific seas and howling winds, the men clung to whatever they could to stay on board.

A rogue wave rose higher and higher above the ship and slammed down, tons of water washing across the deck. One man lost his grip. He was swept into the wild roiling sea. No one knew what to do. No one knew how to save him.

The crew watched wave after wave pulling the man farther and farther from the ship. The crew thought he was lost. But a large black ship dog fearlessly leaped into the frigid water. He sprinted over to the man and caught him before he was swallowed by the waves. The man grabbed on to the dog. The dog fought the seas, the wind, and the blinding spray and pulled him back to the ship.

The dog saved the sailor's life. The dog was known in Italy as a Terranova. The English translation was Newfoundland—the birthplace of this breed.

The story inspired Ferruccio. He thought that Terranovas might be trained to become water rescue dogs. Ferruccio started by working with his own Terranova to see if his dog was trainable.

Quickly he realized his dog instinctively retrieved people from the water. Ferruccio also discovered that Newfoundlands have a body perfectly designed for swimming. Their chest is shaped like the hull of a boat so water flows easily around them. They have webbed paws enabling them to catch more water while swimming. It's as if they are wearing paddles. They have a thick double coat that is water-repellant so they can stay warm in cold water and afterward on land.

Ferruccio said there are many dog breeds trained by the school that instinctively retrieve items and people from the water. There were other dog breeds that did not have the same instincts, but they could be trained to become water rescue dogs. They just had to meet a minimum weight requirement of thirty kilograms—sixty-six pounds. Dogs needed to be large and strong enough to pull people to shore, as the large Newfoundlands were. They could pull six people to shore. A golden retriever or a Labrador could pull in three or four people at a time, and other breeds depending on their size and strength could pull in one or two.

I looked at Mas. She was nine years old and still alert and keen. "Can she pull in six people at one time?"

"Yes, she can. She is powerful and has endurance," Ferruccio responded.

Remembering the way Al greeted Mas, I asked Ferruccio if Mas was working with Al to teach her to become a canine lifeguard. That hit a nerve.

He explained that Al was nearly two years old, and he and Donatella had been working with her since she was a puppy. But Al's progress was incredibly slow. Ferruccio said he started the school nearly twenty-five years ago and Donatella had been working there almost as long. They had trained a lot of dogs, but Al was different from the others. She just didn't get it. Ferruccio was having Mas work with Al, and he hoped Mas would have more success with her than they had.

We walked to the swimming area to meet some members of the school.

6

Little Tails in the Water

There were five puppies. Fluffy little puppies. They were chasing one another on the shore. They were growling, pouncing, barking, tumbling, rambunctiously rolling, and piling on top of one another. Their owners were laughing as they watched their dogs play. They caught them, scooped them up, and carried them into the lake. The puppies were just starting to learn to swim.

From the beach, it looked like they were participating in a mommy-and-me swim class, but instead of moms teaching their babies, men and women were holding their puppies in the shallow water, walking with them, and encouraging them to swim. The puppies were not old enough to participate in the water dog rescue school, but their owners wanted to give them a head start, help them learn to swim so they would be water safe and perhaps attend the water dog rescue school when they grew up to be big dogs.

The puppies' paws were popping high above the water and they were grabbing more air than water, splashing more than swimming, struggling to keep their heads up.

One puppy lost the battle. He suddenly slipped underwater and came up coughing. Fear filled his brown eyes and paralyzed his body. He coughed. Whimpered.

His owner picked the puppy up, held him near his chest while the puppy cleared his throat, and then he set his puppy back in the water. This time he supported his puppy by pushing his belly and chest up so he would stay above the water.

Ferruccio nodded his approval. If the puppy stopped swimming when he was afraid, it would make it more difficult for him to learn the next time he came to the lake. He would have to get over his fear before he could learn to swim.

The puppy was moving his paws faster and flipping his tail out of the water. He was beginning to realize that his tail was attached to him and that he could use it as a rudder. His tail could help him find his balance and allow him to swim in a straight line.

One of the things I enjoy most about watching children and puppies learn to swim is the moment when something clicks inside them. Looks of amazement, excitement, and surprise fill their faces. Suddenly they realize they can use their arms and legs to propel themselves in the water. Children test their hands. Puppies experiment with their paws, move them different ways and at different angles. They feel the water and their own power to move it. And they experience something new that they never feel on land—their own buoyancy. Water suddenly becomes something magical and fascinating.

I remembered when I was a child my parents would fill a sink with water and let my brother and me play in it for hours. We came from a family that had a long history of being swimmers. Maybe we were tapping into our instincts.

Although the water puppies were bred to become water dogs, swimming was challenging. I watched two golden retriever puppies, a German shepherd puppy, and a Newfoundland puppy starting to move in the water. They paddled, hesitated, sank, recovered, paddled faster, and listed.

Their balance and speed were different in the water than on land. It took them longer to move through the liquid, and as they swam, the water reacted to their movement: it flowed around them, pushed, pulled, lifted, and dropped them. The puppies felt what the water was doing to them, calculated the adjustment of their stroke and balance to compensate for the water movement around them. Their small round faces were full of concentration and determination.

A man and a woman were so focused on their puppies that they bumped into each other. Ripples of laughter filled the air.

Standing in the center of the swimming area, a tall, lanky instructor and his large red golden retriever were watching over the puppies and people.

"This is the best work," he said, smiling. The lifeguard dog looked just as happy and engaged with his soft red ears relaxed, brown eyes scanning the lake, mouth open, and the tip of his tongue resting on his lower lip between his two white incisors.

I watched an owner steer his black Newfoundland puppy toward a golden retriever puppy who was held by a slender woman. The golden retriever puppy paddled to the Newfoundland, lifting her head and sniffing his lips. The woman called another owner and he carried his German shepherd and set him down beside the golden retriever and held the puppy in place. The three puppies were lined up with the three owners standing shoulder to shoulder, getting ready to race.

Other owners cleared the water, their dogs and puppies congregating on the edge of the lake where the race would finish. They were having fun, discussing the qualities of the three puppies, and choosing their favorite.

Each puppy had certain strengths. The German shepherd's legs were long, his feet were large, and he was able to reach far in front of his chest and take long, efficient strokes. The Newfoundland was so buoyant that he didn't need to expend energy to keep his head above water; all of his energy went to forward motion. And the golden retriever was a natural; her technique was perfect. She had a feel for the water that enabled her to grab and pull water in a way that was smooth and looked effortless.

But the three puppies also had their weaknesses. The German shepherd became irritated by water splashing in his eyes and ears. The Newfoundland grew tired, and he lost his concentration and his rhythm broke down, so he swam with a stuttering motion, causing him to use more energy than if he maintained a constant speed. Smaller and more delicate than the two male puppies, the golden retriever was distracted by people. She craved their attention.

The puppies dog-paddled in place as their owners held them. The air was crackling with energy and excitement anticipating the competition.

The lifeguard walked to the owners and puppies in chest-deep water and checked to make sure their noses were aligned. He told the owner of the golden retriever to move her dog back.

He raised his arm to signal ready, but before he could drop his arm to signal go, the Newfoundland false-started. The lifeguard called him back.

Laughing and shaking their heads, the owners turned around and repositioned their puppies, as friends from shore teased and bantered with the owner of the New-foundland. He set his dog between the two other puppies.

When they were in position, the lifeguard reminded the owners that they could support their puppies but they couldn't push them through the water, the puppies had to pull themselves, and the first puppy to clear the water won the race.

The lifeguard lifted and lowered his arm before anyone could false start again.

That caught everyone off guard and the puppies looked confused.

The golden retriever snatched the lead. The Newfoundland, who was fond of her, pulled faster to catch up, and the German shepherd extended his legs farther to take longer pulls and to catch up with his best friend, the Newfoundland.

On shore people were shouting, dogs and puppies were barking. People down lake heard the cheering and joined in.

The German shepherd surged ahead and grabbed the lead. The golden retriever slipped to second, and the Newfoundland drifted to third. But the shepherd's lead was only the blink of an eye.

Ten meters from the beach, the golden retriever and Newfoundland pulled ahead, but suddenly the golden retriever slowed to blow bubbles, the Newfoundland fell off pace when he slowed to watch her, and the German shepherd paused to shake the water from his floppy ears.

Cheering and applauding, the crowd urged them to swim to shore.

The golden retriever, Newfoundland, and German shepherd resumed their race.

Five meters from the beach the Newfoundland was sprinting, the golden retriever was skimming along the surface, and the German shepherd was surging forward.

One owner turned to me. "It's like we are racing three Ferraris," he said, grinning.

The owners on the beach were shouting and waving and their dogs were barking and lunging forward as if willing the racing puppies to shore.

The shouting was louder, more intense.

The Newfoundland lunged forward, the golden retriever put her face in the water, lowering her body, anticipating her paws touching the sand. The German shepherd's long legs touched the bottom first, and he pushed off with his hind legs. The golden retriever dolphined beside him, and the powerful Newfoundland bounded out of the water. It looked like the Newfoundland would win, but the German shepherd turned on his speed and ran up the beach dead even with the golden retriever. The finish was so close that the lifeguard thought the Newfoundland won, but he wasn't sure from his angle. It could have been the golden retriever or the German shepherd. Some owners were certain that the Newfoundland finished first, and others applauded the German shepherd and some congratulated the golden retriever. But it didn't matter who'd won; they all had fun.

7

Zen and Tennis Balls

A hot breeze swept across Lake Idroscalo, ruffling the aqua-blue water and making it sparkle like diamonds. It was a beautiful place to spend the day with people and dogs and have fun.

Ferruccio and I walked twenty-five meters along the soft white sandy beach to an area where about a dozen intermediate dogs were training with their owners. Ferruccio said they were working on conditioning. The dogs and their owners had to be strong and in good shape to be able to save people, they needed to have the endurance and strength to swim and pull a person into shore or to a boat, and they needed to be quick so they could swim through a current. The dogs and their owners were wearing swim vests to help them float and keep them safe. They were swimming with their heads up for about twenty-five meters to deep water, turning, and then swimming back to shore. There was something captivating and almost hypnotic about watching them swim in and out in oval patterns.

Each pair of dog and owner swam at their own pace and in their own rhythm. They were working hard, but they were not fighting the water. They were moving across it. It was probably from my years of swimming on teams, coaching swimmers, and watching people swim that I quickly noticed the different ways the dogs swam. The Newfoundlands were the strongest swimmers followed by the Labradors, golden retrievers, flat-coated retrievers, German shepherds, and all the other dogs including the hybrids—mixed breed dogs.

Of all the dogs in the water the golden retrievers looked the most relaxed. They paddled along, back and forth, like they were as at home in the water as they were on land. I imagined putting a bright flowered swim cap with hot-pink, blue, yellow, lime-green, and orange flowers on one golden retriever's head. She was an easygoing girl and she would not have minded. From behind she would have looked like an elderly lady daintily swimming breaststroke high in the water. She would have enjoyed watching the clouds as they sailed overhead and became cats, squirrels, and large white rabbits.

As the dogs and their owners moved toward and away from shore, they mingled with one another and spoke a few words of encouragement. Those long conditioning swims could be grueling, but having a friend to talk with at the end of each lap helped a lot. I remember those years of training and stopping for ten seconds at the end of a lap to say something encouraging or funny to a friend or hoping that they had something to say to me so that I could think about it for the next ten or fifteen minutes or hour before we spoke again. It was often difficult to stay engaged, especially when we were getting tired, and by the looks of it, the dogs and their owners were becoming fatigued and slowing down.

Any good coach knows this is the time to give the swimmers a break and let them catch their breath. Ferruccio knew this and he asked his students—people and dogs—to stop swimming. After a few minutes' break he spoke to them in Italian, introduced me, and asked them to show me how they swam ahead of their dogs. It was fun to see how well they worked together. And most of the dogs knew exactly what to do. They repeated the drills so the dogs would remember. There were a few younger dogs that had recently joined the school and they did not follow their owners very well, but they were starting to learn.

One tall, lean man with wide shoulders spoke English well. He stepped out of the water for a moment to welcome me. I remembered how difficult it could be to swim back and forth for a long period of time and stay focused. I told him that I played water polo, and swimming back and forth with the ball made the laps more fun. I asked if he ever used a tennis ball and had his dog retrieve it.

What he said surprised me. He said that they never use tennis balls. The dogs are learning to retrieve people. Smiling, he said that he has to become the tennis ball. Or he has to become more interesting to a dog than a tennis ball so the dog will retrieve him. They do not play with toys in the water.

"You become the dog's toy?"

"Yes. It's Zen. Almost mystical," he said seriously.

I had not expected that at all, but I did anticipate what was happening in the water. It was near the end of the workout, a time when coaches usually have their swimmers sprint and race one another to have them work hard when they are tired so they will swim faster when they are rested. Sprinting at the end of workouts changes the energy flow and challenges a different physiological system within their bodies. Coaches also have swimmers race at the end of a workout to have teammates cheer for one another and bring the team closer together.

The dogs and owners were almost done with their workout. The owners released three dogs and they formed a pack. Suddenly a red-coated golden retriever decided he was going to be the leader of the pack. He started sprinting. The other dogs felt his energy and that tapped their competitive spirit. A black Newfoundland and a yellow

Labrador started paddling faster than the red retriever and they pulled up on either side of him. They were riding in his slipstream. Dragging off him. Saving energy. Swimming faster. The three dogs were snout-to-snout. Paw-to-paw. Head-to-head. The Newfoundland discovered a burst of energy. He sprinted ahead. But the red retriever wanted it more. He caught the Newfoundland, dropped his head, dug deep, and sprinted to shore.

People were cheering, shouting, laughing, and when everyone reached shore, the owners were petting, hugging, and praising their dogs.

We walked to the last section of the beach where the advanced rescue dogs were training. Some of these dogs had been training for five years or more. They needed to stay in shape and continue training so they would always be prepared.

All the dogs in the advanced group had joined their owners for obedience training. Much of their work was done on shore before they got into the water, on a boat, or in a helicopter.

The owners went through a series of drills. They gave their dogs the signal to sit. The dogs immediately sat. They gave the dogs the command to stay. The dogs stayed. The owners walked a distance and called and signaled their dogs to come. The dogs ran to their owners and were rewarded with hugs and praise. The owners looked into their dogs' eyes and stroked their furry faces.

Ferruccio explained that they used both voice commands and hand signals. The hand signals were important because a dog might not be able to hear a command if there was too much surrounding noise, but a dog could see a hand signal and know how to respond.

All the dogs were wearing harnesses with an attached buoy. The dogs and owners were practicing what they called "the dolphin system." They swam about fifty meters out and the owners grabbed the dogs' harnesses. The dogs towed the owners rapidly to shore. The dolphin system saved the owner's energy when he or she was rescuing a person, and the drill helped build the dog's strength and endurance. It was beautiful to watch dog and owner work together. They were perfectly rehearsed and anticipated each other's movement. They were water dancing. The dog and owner flowed together as they moved toward shore, slid apart when they reached shore, and moved together as they swam back offshore. All while the clear blue water flowed around them, lifting, spinning, and pulling them through its own flow and in its own time.

The day was getting hotter and I was uncomfortably warm and gritty from the long airplane flights. I had never been to Lake Idroscalo and I wanted to feel, see, and experience what it was like to swim in this Italian lake with Mas and see how she performed. As I changed into my swimsuit, I felt a rush of excitement.

I love to swim: solo, with friends, or with dogs. Each experience is unique. When I swim alone close to shore, I let my mind escape the confines of my body. The smooth rhythm of my arm stroke, my light kick, and the sound of the long exhale of bubbles flowing from my mouth and off my fingertips let me mindfully meditate. I observe my sensations, feelings, and thoughts, and as I continue swimming, my mind shifts to movement meditation, where I experience peace through action. My mind wanders from thought to thought and as the water diminishes sound, my meditation becomes spiritual and transcendent. By focusing on the silence around and within me I feel a deeper connection to nature, God, and the universe.

When friends swim with me, my focus is more on them. I enjoy being with them, pacing, pushing one another, moving in unison, joking, laughing, and knowing that we are sharing an adventure. Being with other swimmers helps me keep my mind off myself, from being tired, sore, or discouraged. In some ways it feels like we carry each other and lift each other's spirits as we swim together.

Swimming with dogs is different—far more intense than swimming solo or with friends. Dogs can't stop paddling when they are in the water or they will sink. Body type makes as much difference with dogs as it does with people. Leaner dogs with proportionally longer legs like Vizslas and Weimaraners have to move their legs faster than other dogs to stay afloat, while golden retrievers and Labradors can swim slower. But in any case, dogs are fully absorbed by the action of swimming. They are alert, attentive, and fixated on a goal.

When I swim with a dog, I feel that intensity and that we are sharing a deeper connection as the dog emanates warmth, exuberance, and delight.

Mesmerized by the shifting wind patterns and geometric designs on the water's surface, I stared across the lake. The aqua color of the water reminded me of the Gulf of Aqaba, where I swam between Egypt and Israel and between Israel and Jordan, celebrating the progress of peace between the three countries. The water in the Gulf of Aqaba was hot, thin, salty, and transparent. Swimming in warm water was so different. Every muscle in my body relaxed and I luxuriated in the warmth. I wondered how Lake Idroscalo would feel.

Mas led the way with a spring in her step and we followed her giant paw prints in the white sand.

8

Mas, *Ben Fatto*

After securing a red life jacket on Mas, Ferruccio handed me one. I smiled but I felt self-conscious, and I was not sure how to put it on. I am a good swimmer and never use a life jacket while I am in the water. I have swum across the Bering Strait and through eight-meter swells off the coast of South Africa; I have swum across the English Channel and in the frigid waters of Antarctica. But I realized what I was doing now was different. This time was not about my swimming in a lake. That was not the reason I was there. I was there to train with the dogs, to learn how they found courage, and to understand how they learned to become water rescue dogs. I put on the life jacket.

Wearing life jackets ensured that we would be able to keep our heads above water, making our experience safer. But more than that, Ferruccio said that we needed to train the same way they made a rescue. He would show me how they trained.

He walked with Mas into the water. She gave a gleeful shake of her body, did a little two-step shimmy, slid right in, and started paddling. Ferruccio was wearing a red wet suit and a life jacket, so he was as buoyant as Mas. She dog-paddled while he swam head-up freestyle beside her. It was a beautiful picture—dog and man swimming side by side, with Mas's bear-sized head beside Ferruccio's smaller one.

They swam at a moderate pace, warming up their muscles and getting their bodies adjusted to the water. When they were about seventy-five meters from shore they turned around and swam back. Mas stayed beside Ferruccio, an arm's length away. She knew the routine. He did not need to coach her.

Her head was bobbing in the tiny waves and her dark brown eyes were glistening. She was enjoying the water, and loved being with Ferruccio. By the wide smile on his face, it looked like he was having just as much fun.

Ferruccio held on to Mas's harness and she demonstrated the dolphin system. She pulled Ferruccio to shore and then he asked her to tow him back out to deep water. He repeated the drill with her three times and then climbed out of the water with Mas and told me what to do.

He said I needed to swim about seventy-five meters offshore and signal to Mas that I was in trouble. I needed to lift my arms above the water and drop them to make a splash. Mas and the dogs at the school were trained to respond to this signal. They knew it meant someone was in distress, and they were trained to swim out and rescue them.

The water in the lake was hot—about eighty-four degrees Fahrenheit, or twenty-nine degrees centigrade. It was not what I expected. I thought the water would be refreshing, but it was warmer than tropical. And it felt different. Fresh water feels thinner than salt water. Hot water feels less dense than cold. Being both fresh and hot the water felt thin; it felt more like swimming through transparent watercolor than through opaque oil paint.

And the thin water made the blue, aquamarine, and aqua colors of the lake look lighter and more fluid.

I walked in and felt little resistance to my body. That meant I would have to pull a lot faster than I usually did to swim at my normal pace. That energy expenditure would create more heat in my body and make me even warmer. I wondered how Mas managed the hot water with her thick double coat. I could easily overheat in the lake and I wondered if she felt the same or if she had acclimated to the warm water.

I always enjoy the transition from land to water. I love to feel the water's lift and the way it eases all the aches of body and mind. The water is always a special place to be. In the hot water, my arms and legs are completely relaxed and feel as loose as boiled fettuccini.

Exhaling and then slowly breathing in the fragrant alpine air, I looked up. The azure sky was clear except for some white clouds sailing slowly by. Taking a deep breath, I put my head underwater and immediately escaped all the noises and tension of the day, and I broke free from the weight of the earth. Everything was quiet. Peaceful. All the talk and questions in my head stopped. My mind finally relaxed. I stared into the deep crystal blue world below. I was immersed in a new and distant place.

I surfaced, breathed, and took a couple of strokes freestyle, but I realized I needed to be able to judge the distance of seventy-five meters from shore, so I rolled over on my back and used Mas and Ferruccio as my reference points. If I kept looking at them, I could gauge how far from shore I'd traveled. Looking at them helped me swim in a straight line. I stretched my arms out behind my head, pulled one arm through the water, lifted the other arm up and back, and pulled it through the water. It felt so good to swim backstroke.

Out of the corner of my eye, I saw Al and Donatella. The Newfoundland was running along the shore, dragging Donatella, who was running as fast as her legs could go. She was shouting.

"Al! Al! Al, *fermare!*"—"Al, stop!"

Al did not stop. Focused on something in the water, she was not listening. Donatella was trying to rein her in. Al was increasing her speed and turning hard, heading toward the water. It looked like she was going to drag Donatella fully clothed in with her.

Al and Donatella were less than a meter from entering the water. Donatella was still shouting at her to stop, but the dog would not listen and kept trying to run into the lake.

Ferruccio signaled to Mas. She moved in front of Al and blocked her with her large body. Al tried to steer around her, but Mas intercepted her and held her ground.

Al was whining so loudly I could hear her from far offshore.

When I was seventy-five meters out, I stopped and raised my arms above my head and dropped them to make them splash to send the signal to Mas to come rescue me. Al started barking wildly.

Ferruccio let Mas go and she leaped into the water, pushed quickly off the bottom, and swam as fast as she could.

When she was an arm's length from me, she slowed and began circling. She stared at me with her large brown eyes and studied my face. She swam closer to me and was careful not to scratch me with her sharp nails. She had learned during training that people could be afraid of dogs. She had been trained to keep a distance until the person she was rescuing realized that she was there to help. She recognized that I was not afraid and swam closer, leaned slightly to the right, and presented the handle on top of her harness.

I reached out with my right hand and held on. I thought that she might have difficulty pulling me in because my body was in a vertical position and that increased water resistance, making it much more challenging for her. But it was obvious she had trained for this. She wasn't having any trouble. Her pace was strong and fast. Each stroke Mas took was smooth and efficient. She instinctively had a great feel for the water. Her stroke was not a simple dog paddle, but more like a shortened breaststroke. Moving her legs and wide-webbed paws in a downward and out motion, she got more out of each stroke and swam more powerfully than if she swam dog paddle. Her back legs supported and balanced her body. Breathing easily and regularly, she continued to pull me to shore. Rescuing people was something she had trained for all her life. She loved it and she was the best.

She kept checking on me, turning her head to make sure I was okay.

Al was still barking and had everyone's attention. Dogs and owners had stopped whatever they were doing to check on the cause of the commotion. Dogs stuck their noses up and sniffed the air; they saw the lake and saw Mas with me. Nothing seemed to be out of place except for Al. The other dogs turned back to their owners. I wondered if she had cried wolf too many times.

Ferruccio watched Donatella finally gain control of Al and saw Mas pull me into knee-deep water. It was thrilling. Mas turned and looked at me again, to make sure I was climbing out of the water with her. I was grinning. She had done incredibly well and I was impressed with everything about her. I reached down and petted her and knelt to hug her. She fanned her tail through the air. Al was circling me excitedly, continuing to pull Donatella.

Long white stringy slobber was dripping from Al's mouth and chin, and when she shook, it flew across the beach. She greeted Mas by eagerly licking her across the nose. Mas acknowledged Al, but she walked around me to make sure I was okay.

"What an amazing girl you are," I said. Maybe by my tone she knew I was praising her, but I couldn't be sure.

"How do you say 'great job' in Italian?" I asked Ferruccio.

"Ben fatto," he said and smiled.

"Mas, *ben fatto,*" I said.

She lifted her thick black tail, held it high, and wagged it.

"Brava, Mas," I said.

Al looked at me with bright golden eyes. Holding my gaze, she wagged her thick furry tail and rested her massive brown head on my hip. I petted her.

Ferruccio and Donatella couldn't help but smile at Al. She melted their hearts too.

Looking back at the lake I wished I could jump back in and swim. Mas seemed to understand me. She was staring at the water, glancing at Ferruccio, and then looking again at the water and wagging her tail.

He understood her. And me.

"Would you like to get back in the water?" he asked.

"I would love to," I said enthusiastically.

9

Dragonfly Freestyle

As we started to walk into the water, a cobalt-blue dragonfly darted around us and circled Donatella and Al. Its four gossamer wings turned iridescent blue in the sunshine, and it looked like a magical creature. Flying acrobatically like a tiny biplane, the dragonfly altered the movement of each of its wings and flew straight up, straight down, side to side, hovered and moved back, moved forward and circled again.

The dragonfly seemed like it was trying to decide what to do. It was strange. I had often seen dragonflies fly in pairs and sometimes in swarms when they were hunting and feeding. I had heard about some that flew thousands of miles across the Indian Ocean, but this dragonfly was flying solo. Finally, spreading its wings, it lighted on Donatella's shoulder. Al stared at the beautiful blue bug while it rested.

The dragonfly's eyes were so large they covered most of its head and it looked like it was studying us. Suddenly it flapped its wings and lifted off. Al barked loudly and lunged for it, but the dragonfly spun quickly, dropped, and skimmed the water's surface. Al continued to bark as it flew across the lake.

Donatella tried to quiet Al, but she was agitated, and then she saw Mas, Ferruccio, and me starting to swim offshore. She was upset and desperately wanted to join us. But she had not been behaving well and would not be rewarded with a swim right away. Al needed to stay on shore while Mas was working with Ferruccio and me.

Mas swam between us as Ferruccio and I swam head-up freestyle. I felt uncomfortable wearing the life jacket. My arms were not able to stretch out, but still it was wonderful to feel my body moving through the warm aqua-blue liquid. There is nothing in the world as glorious as swimming.

Ferruccio's stroke was smooth and relaxed. He was completely comfortable in the water. I watched Mas. She was an amazingly agile swimmer. I had my goggles with me and asked Ferruccio if I could put them on and dive underwater to watch Mas swim. I had never seen a Newfoundland's underwater pull.

I tried to swim ahead so I could dive under as Mas was swimming toward me. But Mas immediately noticed my change in speed and she pulled stronger to stay beside me. Ferruccio had to call her so she would continue swimming with him as he slowed our pace. Taking a deep breath, I dove deep and swam under her. She was so aware of everything around her. I wondered if she could feel my air bubbles on her toes. I tried not to let any bubbles escape. I did not want to disturb Mas and have her change her stroke or speed.

The water was fairly clear, a light milky blue. I could see Mas's front paws doing the shortened breaststroke pull. It was so strong and she was kicking equally strongly with her back legs. I watched her front paws again. They looked like huge paddles. The black skin webbing between her large toes enabled her to open her paws and capture so much water with each pull. And I also loved looking at her churning hind legs that powered her through the water. She was designed by nature to be hydrodynamic and the water flowed easily over her body. She did not fight it. She just moved through it. It was a beautiful thing to see.

When I surfaced, I was smiling. I told Ferruccio that I wished I had hands like Mas's paws. I would be able to swim so much faster. He grinned and said it would help me on the water but webbed hands might be difficult to use on land.

We swam until we were a little more than fifty meters

from shore. Ferruccio said he would have Mas do the dolphin system and tow him to shore, then I would signal her to come get me. I asked Ferruccio if she minded working with different people. He said they encourage it. It gives Mas and the other dogs and owners more experience. And sometimes if an owner is having difficulty teaching a dog something, another person can help. I said this reminded me of swimming on a swim team. Sometimes the coach would try to help me make a stroke adjustment and I did not quite understand what he was saying, but a teammate would demonstrate something for me or say something slightly different and I would understand and be able to make the correction.

Mas towed Ferruccio to shore and I lifted my arms and dropped them on the water. Mas turned around and sprinted toward me. Al wanted to come too. She was trying to break free from Donatella. Ferruccio said something to Al and she seemed to calm down.

Mas moved in closer to me this time. She knew I was not afraid of her. She circled and watched me to make sure I grabbed the handle on the harness. When she started swimming, she felt the resistance of my body in the water. I loved the ride. But this time I decided to do something different. I let go of the handle.

Mas stopped. She turned, swam around me, and presented the handle. I held on for about ten meters and let go again.

She stopped, turned, circled faster, and presented the handle again. This time she looked worried. I grabbed the handle and she started pulling faster this time. When we were about ten meters from shore, I let go again. She seemed annoyed with me. She was more insistent when she presented the harness this time and when I held on, she towed me until my stomach touched the sand. When we climbed onto the beach, she did a little happy dance.

Curious about the way Mas responded, I told Ferruccio what had happened. He explained that Mas had been trained for this. Sometimes the handle slipped from a person's hands because the water was rough or they were tired. Mas would continue circling a person until she knew the person was holding on to the harness. By circling back, Mas gave them another chance to be saved.

Al was still waiting for her turn. Ferruccio and Mas swam her out to deep water. Ferruccio held on to Al's harness and Mas swam beside them. Ferruccio alternated between the two dogs. And everything seemed to be going smoothly. Donatella was standing beside me watching Al and smiling. For the first time since we met, she was relaxing. Al was doing what she was supposed to do. She was rescuing Ferruccio. But everything changed when five mallard ducks landed on the lake.

The ducks were swimming about twenty meters from Al. They were distracting her. She heard them quacking and saw them pecking one another. Two of the ducks suddenly turned. They lifted their wings, pressed them down against the air. That lifted them from the lake, and they continued flapping their wings so they could run across the water's surface with their webbed feet, gain speed, and fly.

Quickly Al turned and started to chase them. She was heading out to deep water. Somehow, Ferruccio and Mas managed to sprint and catch her before she caught the ducks.

When we returned to shore, Al's head was hanging low as she climbed from the water. She knew from Donatella's grimace that she was upset with her. Donatella called her and she obeyed, but Al had lapsed. Donatella said that training Al was not as simple, fast, or as straightforward as it seemed. It took "the patience of Job." Donatella immediately snapped a leash to Al's harness.

The puppies were nearby. They had finished their workouts and were running up to Al. She was calm and gentle as she nuzzled them, even though they were so unruly.

Other dogs joined the group. Almost everyone was happy.

There was a feeling of expectation in the air. Owners were watching the dogs. One Labrador twisted her body to one side and lifted her head.

Someone shouted, *"Guarda quello!"*—"Look at that!"

Everyone turned to watch.

Nothing happened.

A golden retriever shifted to one side and turned his head.

"*Guarda quello!*"

Everyone watched.

Nothing happened.

A yellow Labrador turned his head and shook and shook and shook. And the water from her fur coat flew into the air and it went everywhere. It hit the puppies, the dogs, and their owners, and it set off a chain reaction of shaking dogs. When the Newfoundland dogs started shaking, people were laughing and ducking and running out of the way. The spray was hitting everyone and everything.

People were watching to see which dog would start the next chain reaction. The splash from the dogs' coats was like confetti. The dogs, owners, and instructors were celebrating the swim, the training, the day, the time together, and their lives.

The owners praised their dogs, scooped up their puppies, and dried them more thoroughly with towels.

Dogs and people were starting to go off in different directions. Donatella led Al to the car to get a bowl of water.

A young blond woman with delicate features and a dainty yellow golden retriever walked over to me. She said she came to say hello. She was aware I was there to observe water rescue dog training.

I told her that her golden retriever looked pretty. She

had two perfect pink bows on her head just above her ears.

The woman explained that since there were so many golden retrievers in the water it was easier to see her dog when she was wearing the bows. She hoped I enjoyed spending the morning with them.

I had a fantastic time, I told her.

She was happy about that, but she was concerned about something. She said Donatella was a top-notch trainer, but it was unfortunate Al was so difficult. When the other dogs were working, she was in a different world, watching bees pollinating daisies in the grass and butterflies fluttering around flowers.

She explained that she had tried to help train Al, as had other members of the team. They had worked hard with her, but Al was a big problem. She did not pay attention. Other dogs did and they learned. Some were fast learners and gained their water rescue dog certification in one year. But Al was such a poor student she might never earn a certificate.

Donatella and Al were approaching.

"Worse, Al is a terrible embarrassment to Donatella. I don't know why she has kept her this long. She is impossible," she whispered, then said, "*Arrivederci*—See you later." She walked away with her perfectly behaved golden retriever wearing two pink bows.

10

Cheese and Vinegar

W ould you like to join us for refreshments?" Donatella asked.

"Oh yes, I would love to," I said.

The day reminded me of the many times I swam with
friends and how after a long workout we would go for
a meal together. We were fatigued and famished. Our
hunger intensified our sense of taste and smell. It height-
ened the way food felt in our mouths. The texture of food
changed. It felt smoother, crunchier, and creamier. Salty,
sweet, sour, bitter, tart, and spicy flavors were elevated.
Food tasted delicious and robust. We ate and relaxed.
We joked and laughed. Sometimes we discussed our
workouts, how we were doing, what we needed to do to

improve, and what the coach thought of us. We discussed what was happening in our lives and in the larger world. We were filled with ideas after long hours with our heads submerged in the water with no one to talk to. We were eager to share our thoughts. The food, conversation, and time filled us up, and we felt happy and replenished.

Donatella and Al led the way through the park along a path between ancient pines. The trees were more than thirty meters high, and their branches were wide and bushy. Dark green needles shaded us from the searing afternoon sun. A gentle breeze stirred the trees so they started swaying, and as Al walked below them, her swaying bushy tail mirrored their motion.

The breeze carried the scent of pine, wild geranium, and the oily sweet smell of wet dog.

We reached a parking lot. This was the first time I had been to a tailgate party for dogs.

People were taking containers of food and putting them on the back of their cars. Some school members had spread colored blankets on the ground and were sitting down in small groups. The dogs knew the routine. They lay down on the blankets anywhere they chose. Some stayed with their owners. Some went to see friends. Some knew where to go to get special treats.

Al was lying down and sniffing the air, her large black nostrils flaring. Donatella reached over to pet her. "Her real talent is to use her nose, and that is not a characteristic that most Newfoundlands have. I've always thought that if Al didn't work in the water, she would have a great career searching for truffles."

Donatella was setting a large bowl of water beside Al, who was panting and drooling heavily. She looked uncomfortable.

Bob, one of the instructors, pulled a large red cloth napkin from his pocket and wiped Al's mouth.

Al looked up as if she was thanking him and Bob stroked her on the top of her head. Al wagged her tail. They were good friends.

"She's a difficult dog, but she has much promise," Bob said with certainty.

At least Bob is hopeful, I thought.

Bob said that every owner carried these napkins. If a dog drooled, anyone in the group would wipe the dog's face.

Most people are disgusted by dog slobber but there in the park no one seemed to mind. While people were sitting and talking, I watched them reach out occasionally and carefully wipe a drooling dog's face and return the cloth to their pocket.

I had never seen a community of people taking care of one another's dogs this way.

Bob asked if I knew why Newfoundland dogs drooled. He explained that they had loose lips—they didn't seal closed. The dogs were bred to help fishermen off Newfoundland pull their fishing nets in from the Gulf of Saint Lawrence and the Atlantic Ocean. The dogs needed to have loose lips so they could breathe while they were holding a rope or net in their mouth and pulling it into shore.

Bob explained that Ferruccio and other owners dreamed of one day traveling to Newfoundland with their trained dogs to do water rescues.

It is always good to have a big dream and work toward it, I told him.

Bob opened a bag. Inside was an enormous chunk of Parmigiano-Reggiano cheese—a hard pale-yellow cheese, often grated and served on pasta dishes.

Bob carefully pulled out and unwrapped a knife and offered me a piece of the cheese.

"I've never seen Parmigiano-Reggiano look like that; I've only seen it grated. I like it a lot but did not know you could eat a slice of it," I said, astonished.

"This cheese is different from the cheese you buy in the United States. In the United States, some manufacturers add cellulose to their cheese. In Italy the cheese is pure. This Parmigiano-Reggiano has been aged for twenty-four months to give it the best flavor," he explained.

Now I knew why the dogs and friends were staying close. This was all part of the after-training ritual. Bob handed me the piece of cheese. The aroma was much more intense than any Parmigiano-Reggiano cheese I had ever had.

Bob was slicing the cheese for everyone and every dog. The people were oohing and aahing as they nibbled their pieces. The dogs gobbled their slices and stared at Bob and wagged their tails, begging for more. The cheese was delicious. It tasted nutty, fruity, salty, a little granular. I stepped in line behind the dogs hoping to be given more. Bob laughed and after giving the dogs one more sample, he handed me another piece.

"Do you like it?" he asked.

"It's amazing."

He grinned with pride and said he traveled to a gourmet cheese shop outside of Milan to find this special cheese. But it was worth it. He and his friends—furry and without fur—all greatly appreciated and enjoyed it

Bob's friend, a taller man with brown hair and a well-trimmed beard, carefully opened a small dark bulb-shaped bottle and asked me, "Have you ever had Parmigiano-Reggiano with balsamic vinegar?"

"I've never tried it," I said.

He explained that they added balsamic vinegar to the cheese and it was unique. It was from Modena in northern Italy and made from a late harvest of Trebbiano and Lambrusco grapes. The grape juice, skins, seeds, and stems were pressed, cooked until they became concentrated, and then left to ferment and age in oak, chestnut, cherry, mulberry, and juniper barrels to create the vinegar's flavor. As the balsamic aged some of the liquid evaporated and the vinegar became thicker. The older the vinegar, the more flavorful and precious.

Bob tore off a gold label from the small bottle. He pulled the cork, smelled the liquid, and smiled slowly. Closing his eyes, he took in a deep breath and handed the bottle to a friend to smell the vinegar. He did the same and said something with great appreciation and then handed the bottle to the next friend. The bottle was passed from friend to friend with everyone exclaiming how wonderful it smelled.

Bob said, "This balsamic vinegar has been aged for twenty-five years. It's very special. There are much younger vinegars, but this is considered the best. Fine balsamic vinegars are expensive. Would you like to try some on the cheese?"

He poured a dot of the precious dark-brown syrup on a small slice of cheese and handed it to me.

He suggested that I taste the vinegar first with just the tip of my tongue so I could experience the flavor all on its own.

I did. The vinegar had a silky texture, and the flavor exploded in my mouth. It was complex: sweet, smoky, and a little acidic. It had notes of chocolate, cherry, and fig.

"Do you like it?" he asked.

"It's delicious. Unlike anything I have ever tasted," I said, again astonished.

When I tasted the balsamic vinegar with the Parmigiano-

Calypso the black Labrador's first jump from a helicopter into Lake Varese, Italy, with Donatella Pasquale and Ferruccio Pilenga steadying Calypso.

Al's first family with Donatella, right, and a friend. Seventy-day-old Al is the third puppy from the left. Family photo, left to right: El Oso, Al's father, the big dog; Baron, Al's puppy brother; Ruuti, Al's puppy sister; puppy Al; Capri, Al's mother, the big dog on the right.

At six months old, Al is on her first patrol training with an instructor dog on a boat on Lake Garda, off the town of Salò.

At forty days old, Baron, Al's brother, is all played out in the snow in Bruxelles, Belgium.

Newfoundlands Maggie (eight months old) and Al (six months old) starting their boat training. They are sniffing the air and water of Lago Maggiore, smelling the excitement and looking for their owners.

Al (less than one year old) at her first time on the Guardia Costiera 800-class boat, training with Donatella and the Guardia Costiera in the Adriatic Sea off Pescara.

Nine-month-old Al wades into Lake Idroscalo and enjoys the water soaking through her thick coats as she waits for Donatella.

Off the shores of Trieste, Al, fifteen months old, is training with SICS volunteers and the Guardia Costeria in the Adriatic Sea on December 4—Saint Barbara's day. Saint Barbara is the protector for the Italian Coast Guard and Italian firefighters.

Poised and ready, Al and Donatella are doing their first training on a Guardia Costeria boat off the shore of Pescara on the Adriatic Sea.

After all the adventure and training, there is an unbreakable bond. For Al and Donatella, a look is enough to know what each is thinking.

Relaxed Blu, Donatella's twenty-month-old Leonberger, winch training with Mariarita Bregagio, preparing to use the helicopter.

Blu at Treviso earning his SICS certification.

A moment of relaxation for Blu and Donatella on Lake Maggiore after spending the day patrolling with the Port Authority crew. Blu died suddenly eight days later of spleen cancer that no one had detected.

SICS volunteers getting a briefing from the Italian Air Force Search and Rescue Department. Zac the Leonberger, center, is trying to get Alyssha's attention. Alyssha, Donatella's elite world-renowned rescue dog, is calm and relaxed.

Reggiano the flavors changed and made a new combination. The cheese mellowed and became nuttier and the vinegar tasted sweeter and fruitier. I had never thought vinegar could taste like that.

A small woman in her forties with shoulder-length black hair and deep brown eyes appeared with a platter of what looked like biscotti—the crunchy Italian cookies often made with almonds and simple flavors like lemon, allspice, or hazelnut. Italians frequently dip biscotti in espresso or in sweet wine to soften the cookie and absorb the flavors of the liquid. The cheese and vinegar had teased my appetite. I imagined how good the biscotti would taste.

The woman explained that the biscotti were homemade, full of vitamins and healthy ingredients, and they did not contain sugar. They were made with care and with love. She offered me the platter. I took one. On cue the dogs circled around us. And then I realized that the biscotti were not for me. They were for the dogs. She showed me how to instruct the dogs to sit and then I doled out one biscotti to each happy animal. The biscotti were hard and crunchy and the dogs looked at the woman and me with large brown and golden eyes, hoping for more.

I was beginning to understand that eating in Italy was special. People paid great attention to detail, to age, flavor, and taste. They carried over that same awareness to their dogs. They had quality time with their dogs when they were learning, exercising, bonding, eating, and having fun together.

Despite my limited Italian, I understood that they were happy to have me there and they were gracious. I saw their smiles, heard their laughter, and saw how much they loved being with their dogs and how they were eager to share what they loved with me. I was grateful for the day of sharing time with people from a different world who welcomed me into their group and gave me insights into what they loved and how they lived.

11

Biscotti Lion Dog

Donatella invited me to her home to meet Zac, her Leonberger. Known as the "lion dog," it is a breed developed by a man from Leonberg, Germany, by crossing a long-haired Saint Bernard with a Landseer Newfoundland and a Great Pyrenees. The dog was created to resemble a lion. Leonbergers are great family dogs, working dogs, and farm dogs. Zac was elderly. He had a disc problem in his neck and he had hip dysplasia. The balls and sockets in his hips did not fit properly as they had deteriorated, but Zac was a happy dog.

When we walked into Donatella's home, Zac was lying down on the floor, thumping his long bushy tail and trying to lift his head. His face was a black-colored fur mask.

His eyes were dark brown and dimming. Long fur covered his neck and chest like a lion's mane.

"Is it okay if I pet him?" I asked cautiously.

"Of course. He is gentle and he loves people," Donatella said.

Al reached Zac before me and she gently touched noses with Zac.

Wagging his tail faster, Zac sniffed Al's feet to detect where Al had been all day. Zac expanded his investigation and sniffed Al's legs and breath. He probably knew that she had been to the lake and had eaten biscotti.

Donatella opened her bag; she wanted to make sure that Zac got one too. She knelt and handed both dogs a biscotti. Zac ate his surprisingly slowly. Al took hers and consumed it in two chomps.

Donatella slowly rubbed Zac's neck and shoulders. He struggled to lift his head and gaze at her. Oh, how he loved her and she loved him. I think she said he was eight years old. She had owned him since he was a puppy.

Al lay carefully down beside Zac, maybe protectively.

"Are you sure Al is okay with my petting Zac?" I asked.

Donatella said it was fine. Al was not jealous. She just loved to be close to Zac. They were best friends.

I got down on my hands and knees so I didn't frighten the dog and let Zac sniff my hands. His nose was large and black and his breath was surprisingly cool. I reached across his wide chest and gently scratched behind his soft black ears and in his armpits. I knew dogs loved to have something scratched that they could not reach with their paws.

I told Al she was a good girl and studied Zac. It was the first time I had ever seen a Leonberger. Running my hands across his broad chest, I felt the long outer coat and the shorter inner coat. Beneath were muscles that were once strong. His fur was a blend of black, white, caramel, and yellow, highlighted with shades of red.

Donatella had waited two years for her Leonberger to be born. She felt so lucky when she found Zac. She said he had a beautiful coat and heart. She knelt beside him, and Zac struggled to lift his head to lick her.

She stroked his back and told him in a warm voice that he was a *bravo cane*—a good dog.

She loved Zac and Zac loved her. But there was so much sadness in their love.

Al felt it and sighed deeply.

Zac's strength was waning quickly. They all knew he would not live much longer. He knew it too. They all tried to go on with life and only show him their love and kindness.

Donatella got up, brushed fur off her pants, and picked up a thick belt resting on a chair. Zac needed to go outside.

I offered to help, but Donatella said she could manage. She threaded the belt under Zac to lift his hips. I wondered how she was ever going to move a dog that big. He was ungainly and weighed more than she did.

She positioned herself beside Zac, squatted down, and

used the strength of her legs to push up and lift him. He managed to get his front legs under himself. His legs wobbled and he slipped, but Donatella helped him to stand, and they staggered outside together.

Al waited for Zac and watched the door, her golden eyes alert. She knew one day soon Zac would not walk back through the door. But this day Zac did and Al greeted him exuberantly, like her best friend had been gone for a long time. She had to show Zac how much she loved him every moment they were together.

Zac stumbled to a corner of the living room and Donatella slowly released the pressure on the belt. He collapsed and struggled to roll onto his side. Al lay down beside him and rested her paw on Zac's leg.

"Was Zac a water rescue dog?" I asked.

"Zac was one of the best. He saved many lives," Donatella said proudly.

"Why was he such a great rescue dog?" I asked.

"Whatever I asked him to do, Zac would do. He trusted me and I trusted him," she said.

Zac heard his name and whimpered. Donatella looked at him with great affection.

"He is a *cane meraviglioso*—a wonderful dog," she said.

I smiled, but I felt sad. There was such a heaviness in the room and there was nothing anyone could do about it.

I followed Donatella into her small kitchen. It was

strange. All the countertops were bare. There weren't any canisters of flour or sugar, or bottles of olive oil, wine, or water. There weren't any jars of spices or even salt and pepper. No chopping boards. No knives. No trays. Nothing.

It looked like Donatella never used her kitchen. She seemed to enjoy food, and usually people who savor food also like to cook.

Donatella opened a cupboard. There was pasta, rice, and other dry ingredients with labels descriptively written in Italian. She took a jar off a shelf, opened it, and offered me a biscotti. She said the biscotti was made by the same friend who baked for the dogs.

The fragrance of lemon and hazelnut filled the air as I reached into the jar and pulled the cookie out. The biscotti was dipped in dark chocolate.

Al looked up, hoping she could share some of my biscotti.

"Dogs can't eat chocolate. For them it is poisonous, but for humans it is something delicious," she said.

I tasted and heard myself saying, "Mmm."

"You like it?" She smiled.

"That biscotti is amazing and the chocolate is bittersweet," I said.

That taste made me think of the way I was feeling. It was bittersweet seeing Zac struggle while hearing how full his life once was.

Al and Zac were perking their ears and staring at

Donatella. She jumped up, handed them each their own biscotti without chocolate, and the dogs devoured them.

"Do you like to cook?" I asked.

"It is okay, but I don't have much time because of the school and my other work," she said.

"Your kitchen is so neat. I don't see any ingredients or utensils anywhere."

Donatella laughed and said that she had to make her home Al-proof. Having Al was like having a toddler in the house. Anything within reach, she would get into, and if something was beyond her reach, she would stand on her hind legs and jump up and grab what she could. Donatella could not even put bread on top of her refrigerator or Al would get it.

We sat in chairs near a coffee table. It was free of vases, cups, and books and I asked why. Donatella explained that with one wag of Al's tail, she could sweep everything on the table onto the floor. Donatella had hoped she could train her not to do this, but she never learned.

Al sauntered into the room. Her big brown head filled Donatella's lap. She looked at Donatella with love and adoration. She was not the dog her owner wanted her to be, but Donatella loved Al and she said her name with warmth as she scratched her firmly on the shoulder. Sighing with pleasure, the Newfoundland turned her head for Donatella to scratch the other side. She worked her way down the back of Al's neck and Al blissfully closed her eyes, leaning heavily against Donatella.

Donatella said that every puppy is a challenge. You never know what the adventure will be. Every dog is a world of its own, with its own character.

Al sighed as Donatella explained that Newfoundlands are big, peaceful, and benevolent dogs. Each breed has its characteristics and histories, but there are always exceptions. Their ancestors were the Molossus, a type of large dog bred to be hunters or protect sheep. These dogs originated in the ancient kingdom of Molossus, which is now western Greece.

Across the living room were photographs of Donatella with a brown Newfoundland. The dog in the photo looked like Al. I walked over to the photo to take a closer look. Donatella was beaming. Her brown eyes were bright and she looked proud beside the Newfoundland, who was gazing confidently into the camera. The dog's mouth was open, and it looked like it was smiling. There were more photos of Donatella and the dog. In each photo they were receiving first place awards. Below the pictures in a case were numerous trophies, silver cups, and plaques.

"What are these awards for?" I asked.

"Obedience," Donatella said.

"Did you and Al win these awards?" I asked.

She glanced at Al, unable to mask the disappointment in her eyes.

"No. Alyssha won all of them," she said.

"She looks a lot like Al. She has the same golden eyes and beautiful brown coat," I said.

"Yes, I got Al because she looks a lot like Alyssha and I thought she would be like her. Alyssha was a real champion," Donatella said.

Al opened her eyes as she recognized Alyssha's name. Unconsciously Donatella stroked Al's head.

"Alyssha was world-famous," she fondly recalled and then said that sadly Alyssha had passed away.

They had traveled throughout Italy for obedience competitions. And Alyssha had been one of the world's best water rescue dogs. Media from around the globe interviewed Donatella and Alyssha. Donatella showed me videos from television stations around the world: RAI (Italy), NHK (Japan), BBC (UK), CBC (Canada), and some clips from television stations in the United States. Alyssha was perfectly well-behaved and incredibly responsive to Donatella's commands.

"Alyssha loved to perform and she loved the spotlight," Donatella said definitively.

Al wandered into the kitchen and checked to see if there was any food. Standing on her hind legs, holding the counter with her front paws, she scanned the countertop for food. Nothing there. She wandered to the sink, jumped up, and stuck her head inside. No food there either.

Donatella called her, then got up to check. She could not trust Al alone for very long.

Standing up to stretch, I noticed the steps that led

upstairs to the bedrooms. They were made from golden brown wood. Looking closer, I noticed that each step was inlaid with a portrait of Alyssha.

I pointed to the steps. "That is a work of art."

Donatella said she was delighted with the work. It had been her idea, but it took a while to find a carpenter with the skill to create the steps with Alyssha's profile. She wanted wood that matched the color of Alyssha's fur. After months of searching, the carpenter managed to find it.

She looked at the steps every day and they reminded her of Alyssha and what a champion she had been.

"Did Al know Alyssha?" I asked.

"I got Al when Alyssha was slowing down. I hoped that having a puppy around would give Alyssha more energy. I also thought Alyssha could help me teach Al. She was a patient teacher, but Al was far too much of a puppy. She chewed on Alyssha's paws, pulled on her ears, and pounced on her."

I asked Donatella if Al was still a puppy.

Donatella said with complete frustration that Al was almost two years old and that she should be minding much better than she was.

When Donatella spoke about Alyssha there were pauses of pain between her words. Sometimes Donatella's voice tightened. Her words trailed off and became a whisper. Her eyes expressed her emptiness. She wanted Al to be like Alyssha. But she was different. She would never be

Alyssha. Donatella tried not to show her disappointment to me, but she mentioned that she had big challenges in her life, and Al seemed to make everything worse. Al would not mind her, but Donatella kept working with her. She hoped that Al would one day become the dog she thought she could be.

Al heard the disappointment in Donatella's tone and saw it in her gestures. She was not the golden dog Alyssha or the lion dog Zac. She was not the dog Donatella wanted her to be. Al knew that, but she loved Donatella anyway.

There was a knock at the door and Donatella opened it. A shiny black Labrador bounded into the room followed by her owner. The Labrador raced across the room and tap-danced around Donatella like Ginger Rogers. Her toenails clicked loudly on the floor. She leaped up on her hind legs to hug Donatella and did a soft-shoe shuffle. As Donatella held her, she glided backward slow-slow, quick-quick-slow, and danced the foxtrot. Donatella was smiling. She signaled the Lab to get down. She immediately sat but was still filled with so much energy. She could not contain herself. She was wiggling wildly.

"Bella!" Donatella leaned over and picked the dog's head up in her hands and rubbed her furry cheeks.

Bella loved the attention. She seemed to melt into Donatella's hands and slammed her tail against the floor.

When Donatella released her, Bella jumped up and zig-zagged between Zac and Al, greeted them, touched their noses, sniffed them, and circled back to her owner. She was so happy to see everyone. She charged the energy of the room. Zac was lying on his side slowly wagging his tail, and Al was alert and watching for her next move.

Once Bella stopped and took a breath, her owner said hello, shook hands, and said goodbye. He was leaving for the weekend and Bella would be staying for a sleepover.

Hoping to find crumbs on the floor, Bella, in typical Labrador fashion, raced into the kitchen, sniffed an empty dog bowl, took a gulp of water from a neighboring bowl, raced over to Zac, and stood over him. She let him sniff her feet and legs so he could explore the worlds she had visited. Zac closed his eyes, savored the scents, and got an aromatic history of Bella's day.

Bella gingerly walked around Zac, dropped down, and rolled onto her side. Making a playful sound, a sort of gurgle growl, she rolled over and looked at Zac upside down. Zac gurgle-growled back at her. She made everyone's day brighter.

Bella reminded me of Cody, my yellow Labrador. He had the same joie de vivre as Bella. He was a people dog. I adopted him from a neighbor when he was six years old. Everyone in the neighborhood knew Cody. Everyone loved him and he loved everyone. He walked through the neighborhood holding his leash in his mouth. That made people smile, which thrilled him. He lifted his head and tail higher and wagged it faster when he saw anyone.

If a neighbor left a garage door open, Cody would walk

right in to say hello. If a neighbor left the front door open, Cody would walk into the house before I could catch him.

Neighbors would shout, "Oh Cody!" like he was a long-lost friend. They were thrilled to see him.

One day Cody ran into a neighbor's house and into the kitchen, where the neighbor was preparing lunch. He heard a refrigerator door squeak open and slam shut. Apologizing, I followed him into the house, calling him. The neighbor asked me if his son could give Cody a biscuit.

As he handed Cody a treat, the son declared, "Cody's not your dog, he's the neighborhood's dog."

He was that and much more. He was our family dog. He loved to watch football and basketball games with my dad, and when my dad cheered his teams, Cody would jump up and wag his tail. He liked to lie beside my mom when she was standing at her easel working on a painting. He loved to sit beside her on the floor when she was working on her needlepoint. And he loved to go for rides in my Mazda Miata with the window rolled down so all people could see was his big yellow head in the window, and he loved to see them pointing at him and laughing because it looked like he was the only one in the car. He loved to swim with me in lakes or in the Colorado River and in the ocean. He was smart and intuitive. Bella had the same characteristics, and she seemed to anticipate whatever Donatella was going to ask her to do.

I said to Donatella that it seemed Labradors responded much more quickly than Newfoundlands. Donatella agreed and said if she told Alyssha to do something, it took a moment for her to respond. If she told Bella to do something, she responded immediately. Both dogs were equally bright and responsive, but Alyssha seemed slower because she was a much larger dog. Donatella hoped that Bella would be a good role model for Al, who was often painfully slow to respond.

12

Dogs Under the Table

Leaving Al behind, Donatella drove me to a nearby trattoria to meet with Ferruccio and Roberto, his friend and fellow instructor, for dinner. We did not talk much along the way. Donatella seemed focused on other thoughts. She mentioned that she and Bob, another instructor from the school, were taking Al to Genoa in the morning. They were planning to meet with the Guardia Costiera to put Al through a test. She invited me to join them. She had mentioned this trip when we spoke on the phone when I was in California. I said then that I would love to go, but she now appeared conflicted and stressed. Maybe it was challenging for her to translate Italian to English for me.

She parked the car and we walked into a cozy restaurant with small tables covered by white tablecloths. Delicate vases with yellow roses and dark green ferns adorned each table and small white candles lit the room with warm amber light. As we walked through the restaurant, a server opened the kitchen door. The aroma of garlic, rosemary, and warm bread floated in the air. It smelled delicious.

Sitting at tables were people who looked like locals. Women were in summer dresses and men in light-colored shirts and pants.

Donatella weaved between the tables, stopping to ask if I would mind sitting outside.

It was warm and calm and the sky was clear blue. Silvery-green-leafed olive trees framed the patio and long strands of white lights hung from their branches. Donatella explained that Ferruccio and Roberto planned to bring their dogs and there was not enough room for them inside the restaurant.

They were waiting for us at a table, and Roberto said he thought I would enjoy this trattoria. It was one of their favorites. The owner was a friend and a big fan of the lifeguard dogs. He always reserved a special table for them. They also selected this restaurant because it served food made from local and regional recipes and seasonal vegetables. It was farm-to-table dining.

Sitting in the open air, talking about dogs and Italy, and enjoying delicious food sounded perfect to me, but

I was so focused on where we were going to sit that I did not notice the three Newfoundlands lying down by the other side of the table. Mas was on the floor beside Ferruccio and there were two beautiful black-and-white Newfoundlands beside Roberto. Resting on their bellies to feel the coolness of the tile floor, they looked like giant bear rugs.

"We hope you don't mind if the dogs sit near the table," Roberto said with some hesitation.

"Having a dog under the table makes me feel like I'm at home." I smiled.

"Really? I thought Americans did not like having dogs around their table," he said, surprised.

"My family always had dogs, and they were always under the table at dinnertime. I had a Dalmatian named Beth, and if we had liver for dinner, I sneaked it under the table for her. I had to do it carefully and hope that she did not make too much noise when she ate it or I would get in trouble."

Roberto grinned and said that when the school members come for dinner the entire area is filled with dogs. They are all over the place, under and around the tables. His two black-and-white dogs were a special type of Newfoundland called Landseers. They were finer-boned with softer fur. They were named after Sir Edwin Landseer, who painted a classic picture of the Landseer dog.

"Their temperament is like the black or brown Newfoundland breed. They are sweet, gentle giants and great swimmers," Ferruccio explained.

Ferruccio began telling stories of three famous Newfoundland dogs. Boatswain was a Landseer given as a puppy to George Gordon Byron, Lord Byron, when he was fifteen years old. Lord Byron was one of England's greatest poets and is famous for swimming across the Hellespont, now known as the Dardanelles. Boatswain and his owner were deeply attached. Lord Byron traveled everywhere with Boatswain and would spend hours drifting in a boat on the lake on his estate in Newstead Abbey reading beside his beloved dog. To test Boatswain's fidelity, Byron would suddenly jump into the water, and Boatswain would leap in after him and drag him to shore.

When Boatswain was bitten by a rabid dog in 1808, a vaccine was not available to save him, but Byron nursed and hand-fed Boatswain, unafraid of being bitten and contracting rabies.

It broke Lord Byron's heart when Boatswain died. He created a monument to the Newfoundland and wrote the heart-wrenching "Epitaph to a Dog" to honor him:

> *Near this Spot*
> *are deposited the Remains of one*
> *who possessed Beauty without Vanity,*
> *Strength without Insolence,*
> *Courage without Ferosity,*

and all the virtues of Man without his Vices.
This praise, which would be unmeaning Flattery
if inscribed over human Ashes,
is but a just tribute to the Memory of
BOATSWAIN, a DOG,
who was born in Newfoundland *May 1803*
and died at Newstead *Novr 18th 1808.*

There is something wonderful about Newfoundland dogs. They are devoted and brave and sagacious.

President Thomas Jefferson commissioned Meriwether Lewis and William Clark to conduct their extraordinary expedition to explore and map the Louisiana Purchase, the land acquired from France in 1803. Jefferson wanted them to find a water passage through the West to the Pacific with the hope of opening trade with Asia. He encouraged Lewis and Clark to meet with Native Americans to learn about their lives, languages, and cultures and encourage trade with them.

Lewis needed a special dog to be a member of the team. He wanted a dog that was large and a powerful swimmer. The expedition would travel across dangerous, unexplored lands and waterways of the western frontier. The team needed a dog that would alert them to danger and protect them. Lewis also experienced bouts of severe depression that often left him bedridden and he needed a constant companion.

Meriwether Lewis traveled to Pittsburgh, Pennsylvania,

to find Seaman, and the dog proved to be a great asset to the team. He hunted with William Clark and drove beavers from their lodges. Clark shot them to feed the team of forty-five men and one woman, Sacagawea, a Lemhi Shoshone who served as an interpreter for the expedition.

Clark admired Seaman and his ability to hunt and share. One day when they were traveling along a river, Seaman saw a herd of pronghorn antelope swimming nearby. He charged into the water, swam over to one antelope, and drowned it. Seaman swam back to shore with it and gave it to Clark, providing much-needed food for the entire expedition.

But in May 1805, when Seaman was retrieving a wounded beaver from the water, he was bitten. The beaver's bite struck an artery, and Seaman nearly bled to death. Lewis conducted emergency surgery and managed to stop the bleeding, saving Seaman's life. Ten days later Seaman saved Lewis and others.

The expedition team had set up camp for the evening and were sleeping outside. Before the sentry could alert the men to danger, an enormous male bison raced through the camp, passing dangerously close to the men and nearly trampling them.

The bison continued racing through camp and was heading for Lewis's tent. Seaman bravely chased the charging animal, forcing him to turn away. He saved Lewis and others that night, and he continued to be their trusted watchdog.

One night Seaman was restless, barking constantly; this was not his normal behavior. The men understood that something was wrong. In the morning they realized that Seaman had tried to warn them that a bear had come within ten meters of camp and eaten their supply of bison suet hanging from a pole.

Seaman also served as an ambassador to the Native Americans, who had little if any exposure to Anglo-American culture. Lewis said they were curious about Seaman and they admired his courage.

Lewis was fond of Seaman, and it pained him to see his dog suffer hardships along the trail. When Seaman walked between the men, prickly pear cactus growing along the ground stuck into his paws. He chewed them and pulled out the large spines, but the smaller ones stung as he walked. He yelped in agony. On July 15, 1806, Lewis wrote his last journal entry about Seaman, describing how he howled from the pain experienced when swarms of mosquitoes bit him.

In spite of many other challenges, Seaman and Lewis and Clark traveled up the Missouri River to its headwaters and reached the Pacific Ocean via the Columbia River. They explored what would become sixteen of the United States. Over a period of two years, four months, and ten days, Lewis and Clark and Seaman would travel more than eight thousand miles across the North American continent and back.

In 1819, when the official account of the Lewis and Clark Expedition was published, Timothy Alden, a clergyman and member of the New-York Historical Society, wrote about Seaman. In his *Collection of American Epitaphs and Inscriptions with Occasional Notes,* he included the text on a dog collar that was in a museum in Alexandria, Virginia. The inscription read, "The greatest traveller of my species. My name is SEAMAN, the dog of captain Meriwether Lewis, whom I accompanied to the Pacifick ocean [*sic*] through the interior of the continent of North America."

Alden noted that Seaman was still wearing the collar when he returned from the west coast of America.

Seaman's fidelity and attachment to Lewis were extraordinary. After Lewis passed away, Seaman would not part from his remains for a moment, and no one could move Seaman from the spot where Lewis was buried. Seaman refused any food offered him, pined away, and died from grief on Lewis's grave. He was always Lewis's best friend.

Another famous Newfoundland was actually from Newfoundland. Hairy Man was part of a daring rescue. On July 10, 1828, the *Despatch,* a large brig sailing from Derry, Ireland, to Quebec, Canada, with two hundred passengers and eleven crew, was caught in a ferocious storm. Ice, gale-force winds, and fierce seas made navigation extremely difficult.

Near Isle aux Morts on the southwest coast of Newfoundland, the brig struck a submerged rock and broke up rapidly. Captain Lancaster and some passengers were drowned when a massive wave swamped one of the lifeboats.

Three days later, Ann Harvey, a seventeen-year-old girl, and her father, George, were fishing nearby. Ann noticed a keg and a bed floating in heavy seas and realized that there had been a shipwreck. She and her father ran home to alert her younger brother and Hairy Man, their Newfoundland.

The Harveys launched their dory and rowed into heavy seas through tremendous swells. After two hours of exhausting effort, they found a group of survivors clinging to the rocks of a tiny island five kilometers from the mainland. The waves and storm surge were so great and threatening that George could not get the boat closer than thirty meters from the rocks.

Hairy Man jumped into the terrifying waves and swam to the rocks, where he grabbed a piece of wood in his mouth and carried it back to the dory. The Harveys tied a rope to the wood and Hairy Man swam it back to the stranded people so they could create a lifeline to get to the dory. They were pulled aboard and rowed to shore.

For three days the Harveys returned to the shipwreck many times and saved 163 people. They took the survivors home and fed them all their winter provisions.

For their extraordinary life-saving efforts the Harveys received a bravery award from the Royal Canadian Humane Association.

The memory of the Harvey family and Hairy Man continues today. In 1987 the Canadian Coast Guard commissioned a ship named *Ann Harvey* that is used for buoy tending, ice breaking, and search and rescue along the Canadian coast.

As Ferruccio finished his stories and we returned our attention to the meal, I realized that dining in Italy was different from eating in the United States. We would be served at least three courses. Dinner would take two hours, possibly three, maybe more, giving us time to relax and enjoy good food and a long conversation. Donatella was listening, but her eyes looked like she was far away and thinking about something else. She said something rapidly in Italian to Ferruccio and Roberto and mentioned Zac and Al and said "*domani*—tomorrow." She explained that she had a lot to accomplish before we traveled to Genoa in the morning and should go, but Ferruccio and Roberto convinced her to stay for dinner.

13

A Toast and Beans

Ferruccio offered a toast: "*Salute.*"

Raising our small glasses, we answered "*Salute*" and sipped sparkling wine. It was from the Franciacorta region. Grown locally in glacier-scoured soil, the grapevines absorbed the essence of the earth and flourished in the summer sunshine. The color of the wine was different from any I had seen—pale yellow with light green tones. It was slightly sweet and fruity like crisp yellow apples, peaches, and apricots.

We sipped the wine and Roberto asked me about the Southern California Newfoundlands. Before we met, they thought this was my first experience with Newfoundland dogs, but I had told them that I often babysat three of them for friends in California.

Jaculin and Brian, my friends, had two Landseers, one named Pork, the other named Beans. Pork was male and Beans was female.

The men thought it was strange that someone would name their dogs Pork and Beans. It was odd. They looked uncertain. Ferruccio asked Roberto to translate what I said again to make sure he understood me. He asked if it was common to name dogs in the United States Pork and Beans. Wasn't that something Americans eat from a can? Their faces tightened. They scowled and looked perplexed. They were more familiar with dignified names. Most dogs in Italy were named after people of importance and places of note.

Pork and Beans were unusual names for dogs, I agreed.

Roberto chuckled and asked, "Why would someone name their dogs after canned food?"

Ferruccio grinned. He translated their names in Italian, "Maiale *e* Fagioli," he said and tightened his lips trying to suppress his laughter. But when he saw me smiling and heard Roberto's belly laugh and saw tears running down his cheeks, Ferruccio burst into laughter. Between laughing and catching his breath he tested more humorous names.

"Parma, Prosciutto, *vieni*," he said. "Ham, Dried Ham, come."

"Fagioli," he said between ripples of laughter.

Finally, I caught my breath and explained that I had asked Brian the same questions. He said the names made people smile. Pork and Beans complemented each other like good friends. He gave them unusual names because he wanted them to be distinctive.

For a moment Ferruccio and Roberto grew serious. They understood the importance of making sure they were clear when they spoke to their dogs, especially in situations when they were involved in water rescues. They thought it was clever that Brian would give them such unique names.

Ferruccio asked me to tell them more about Pork and Beans.

Jaculin and Brian lived in Emerald Bay, an idyllic beachside community in Southern California. Everyone in the neighborhood knew Pork and Beans and Otis, their older sibling who was an enormous black Newfoundland. Traveling anywhere with them was challenging. The dogs were huge celebrities. When neighbors saw the three dogs outside, they would immediately stop whatever they were doing to say hello.

The dogs loved attention. They would gently sniff the little children, let them pet them and hug them. They carefully encircled children so all that could be seen were the huge dog faces and tiny faces of laughing kids. The dogs would try to lick the children and were careful not to knock them over. Being with them and watching the way people responded was like listening to Beethoven's "Ode to Joy"—a celebration of unity and humanity.

When Brian and Jaculin left on a trip, they calmly said goodbye to their dogs. After they drove away, the dogs followed me everywhere. It was not out of a sense of anxiety. They just wanted to see what I was doing. They were extremely curious and seemed so well-behaved.

When I prepared their meals—a mixture of lean ground beef, cooked oatmeal, and special vitamins—they sat patiently.

Donatella asked how often they were fed and I told her twice a day. Donatella said that Al ate at seven a.m. and seven p.m. and was fed a protein food so she did not have to change her diet when she traveled, which would stress her body. The Canadian dog food she bought was distributed all over the world.

She added that Al had a voracious appetite and vacuumed up her food, so Donatella could not feed her in a smooth bowl; she had to put Al's food in a three-cylinder container to slow her consumption. She would eat anything but bananas and anything with that texture. She didn't have any problem eating with other dogs because in the time it took to count to five she would have finished her meal. She could eat right beside another dog and there wouldn't be any problem.

I asked Donatella if she ever gave Al prosciutto, salami, or pancetta as a special treat. Donatella, Roberto, and Ferruccio shook their heads.

Ferruccio said they never fed their dogs Italian cold cuts

because they were full of sodium and they could damage their dogs' kidneys, and he asked how much ground meat I fed Otis, Pork, and Beans.

I said I gave them about a large handful of the meat and oats mixture.

After Otis, Pork, and Beans finished eating, I brushed them. Each waited for their turn and luxuriated in the attention. They sighed as I brushed the loose fur off their shiny coats and they snuggled close to me when I ran my hands around their faces and over their bodies to check for foxtail seed and other grass seeds that could burrow into their skin and cause infections.

Every day I was with them I worked on my first book, *Swimming to Antarctica,* and the dogs stayed with me. They kept me company and it felt like they were watching over me.

Ferruccio was listening closely to me and said, "That is how Newfoundlands are."

I continued with my story. Beans lay near the desk by my feet. Pork rested just beyond her, and Otis lay partly in the doorway to the office and partly in the hallway. They were sentries. No one could enter or leave the room unless the dogs let them pass. They would open their eyes often and scan the area. I felt safe with them.

The dogs needed a lot of exercise to work off energy and stay physically and mentally healthy. We took a long walk each morning when it was cool and another one in the evening. I hooked them up to their leashes and let them choose the direction. They always chose a path that went through the residential area toward the beach, and they were well-behaved. But one day, I decided to take them on a more inland route so they would not be bored and I could explore more of the community.

When they realized that we were taking the inland route, Otis, Pork, and Beans started huffing and puffing and hyperventilating with excitement. I should have expected something was going to happen.

We started our walk at a brisk pace, and when we reached a fork in the road and took the left branch, the dogs lifted their heads, perked their ears, and raised the fur on their backs to make themselves appear larger. I sensed they were preparing for something big and threatening, but I did not see any signs of trouble. No one was on the street. No dogs or cats were roaming free, and there was no mail truck or mail carriers in the area.

Then in the distance, I heard a muffled bark.

The dogs heard it. They started walking faster and they pulled me harder.

I told them to wait in a commanding voice.

They slowed to a trot and I thought I had them under control. We continued walking with Otis in the lead and Beans and Pork on either side of him, but as we turned a sharp corner, a barrage of loud, snarling barks erupted from somewhere ahead of us. Otis barked once to signal a charge. The three dogs lunged forward, nearly ripping their leashes from my grasp.

I grabbed the leashes with both hands and held on as tightly as I could. The dogs were breathing hard and fast. I was stumbling behind them trying to catch my breath. I told them to stop, but they did not obey. They continued pulling me. Just like Al with Donatella.

Otis, Beans, and Pork were running toward a pale-yellow Spanish-style mansion. A white-colored cairn terrier leaped from the top step of the doorway and ran to the gate.

Otis, Pork, and Beans saw the white flash and started running faster. The cairn terrier was leaping up and down the steps, barking so hard he had to stop and catch his breath. I could not understand why a dog that small would agitate three Newfoundlands.

I shouted their names, but they only seemed to hear the terrier.

Climbing to the top step to make sure his voice carried farther, the terrier barked and barked and snarled.

Otis, Pork, and Beans were infuriated by the terrier's barks, and it had become their single mission to silence him.

I was shouting at Otis, Pork, and Beans, telling them to stop and sit, but they did not hear me. I had to figure out how to control the three Newfoundlands. I couldn't believe my feet could move so fast. I was breathing hard, my lungs felt like they were on fire, and sweat was running down my face.

The cairn terrier released a barrage of barks and Otis,

Beans, and Pork snapped into a faster gear. I stumbled and fell, but I would not let go of the leashes. I did not want the dogs to get loose and hurt the terrier. I arched my back and lifted my head to keep my face from scraping across the asphalt.

It was strange. At first it was fun. It was like being a child again, sledding headfirst down a snowy hill at full speed, being on the edge of control and watching the world fly by like it was on fast-forward. But that exhilaration only lasted a few moments. Having absorbed the heat from the morning sun, the asphalt was hot, and the friction caused by my body moving across the pavement burned through my clothes. The road tar smelled sickly sweet and my perception of space, time, and distance was altered. The road that I had driven on that had appeared flat to me was now sloped. Unnoticeable cracks had become wide chasms, and gentle depressions became large potholes. Patches of shattered white and green glass, sharp twigs, hard pebble-sized eucalyptus seeds, and abrasive sand hurt me. Scraping along the road was becoming very painful. Telling Pork, Beans, and Otis to stop was not working.

It is amazing how quickly the mind can work, how fast it can bring forth a multitude of memories, sort through them, and mine them for vital information. I suddenly remembered Martin Buser, a friend who won the Iditarod four times with his champion sled dogs.

14

Focaccia and the Iditarod

I paused in telling the story. Focaccia arrived wrapped in a white towel nestled in a wicker basket. Ferruccio peeled the cloth back and the aroma of steamy bread wafted up into the evening air. We passed the basket and breathed in the delicious fragrance of rosemary and the fresh smell of salt. I selected a small rectangle and waited for Robert and Ferruccio to take slices. I bit into the focaccia. It was warm, delicate, soft, and slightly chewy.

I continued the new story. Martin Buser lives in Big Lake, Alaska, but was born in Winterthur, Switzerland. He is strong, lightweight, and compact like an endurance runner. On a beautiful Alaska summer's day, he invited me to join him and his team on a training ride.

We met at his home and walked along a dirt road to the kennel. One dog heard our approach and howled a rising, loud "Awhooo." Sustaining the howl for nearly ten seconds, the dog had a voice that carried far and wide across the wilderness. Martin's lead dog was alerting the team that we were approaching. A second dog echoed, "Awhooo." It sounded like a wolf. The whole team of dogs answered in a chorus of howls. It was the call of the wild.

The hairs on the back of my arms stood up. There was something breathtakingly beautiful and haunting in their voices. The sound connected the dogs to the earth and sky and all the wilds of Alaska.

Martin led me through the kennel. The dogs looked different from the Alaskan huskies most sled dog racers in Alaska choose. Martin's dogs had shorter hair and brown eyes instead of blue. They were distinct—the offspring of a perfect cross between a German shorthaired pointer and an Alaskan village dog. Martin believed that this pairing would enable him to develop and train dogs that were born with genes for speed and endurance. He thought this combination of qualities could help them win the Iditarod.

Other sled dog racers thought Martin was making an enormous mistake. They did not believe that Martin's shorter-haired dogs could survive the frigid winter nights when the temperatures plummeted to minus one hundred degrees Fahrenheit (minus seventy-three degrees centigrade). They thought it was impossible for Martin's dogs to succeed. Martin gradually acclimated his puppies to the cold air, like open-water swimmers acclimate to cold water over the months and years before a big swim. He and a friend trained the dogs, worked with their speed, and built their endurance. Martin did what others thought was impossible. He and his dog team won the Iditarod and set the record for fastest time.

We reached the sled and I climbed on. Martin stood behind me to drive. Seven dogs were stretched out ahead of us. Some of these dogs would be on teams that would win the Iditarod. I could see just over their heads. Martin signaled the lead dog to go.

We rode so close to the earth that grasses, flowers, and bushes that were ankle high when I was walking were now flying past my shoulders. The dogs ran with boundless energy and exuberance. It seemed like they could run forever.

Martin told me that a good lead dog was curious, always wanting to finish what he started, and had heart. He led the team and the team followed.

I was remembering my experience with Martin and his dogs as I was being dragged along the ground in Southern California. I realized Otis was the lead dog. If I could get Otis's attention, and get him to stop, Pork and Beans would follow.

I shouted and shouted at Otis to stop. He paused. He

was still focused on the terrier, who was launching himself into the air, pulling his legs into his body so he could pound the gate and torment Otis, Pork, and Beans even more.

I continued shouting at Otis, and suddenly he came to a full stop. The others stopped too and Beans sniffed my head and licked my face with her hot, sticky tongue. Pork sniffed and tickled my ears with his whiskers, and Otis nudged my shoulder with his snout. I felt embarrassed that I had not been able to control the dogs, but they finally listened. And later when I told Brian about our outing, he said the dogs hated that terrier.

Ferruccio reminded me that ultimately, the three dogs listened to me. Often it was difficult to control just one Newfoundland.

Donatella nodded and attempted a smile. It seemed that her thoughts were elsewhere.

15

Aperitivo and Rattlesnakes

The server arrived with tiny plates of black and green olives, hard salami from Genoa, Bagòss di Bagolino (white cheese from Lombardy), crunchy walnuts, and a tiny bowl of local honey. We took our time and enjoyed the food. Ferruccio asked if there were other adventures with the three Newfoundland dogs in Emerald Bay.

I was happy to continue stories about the California Newfoundlands. While I couldn't be sure that Ferruccio fully understood me, I think he grasped most of it.

I told them I took Otis, Pork, and Beans for a light hike on the trails in the hills above the houses. It was in early spring and the area was glorious. Bright orange California poppies, blue and purple lupine, and woolly sunflowers were blooming. The days were still cool, but the sun was warm and the rocks concentrated that heat. Spring is when southern Pacific rattlesnakes emerge from their winter hibernation and become active. They enjoy the warmth of the rocks and sunshine. Southern Pacific rattlesnakes live in the hills above Brian's home and can also be found in the westernmost counties of Southern California and on Santa Cruz and Santa Catalina Islands. These rattlesnakes are large and very poisonous. They grow from one to three meters long. They range in color from dark brown to gray, and the back of their chubby body is marked with dark-rimmed blotches. The snake has a triangular head, elliptical catlike pupils, hooded eyes, and a stubby tail with a rattle at the tip, which it shakes as a warning to scare off intruders.

The snake is dangerous and with its bite injects a neurotoxin into a person or animal that can cause difficulty breathing, loss of coordination, and coma. I wondered what the chances were that we would encounter a rattlesnake on the trail.

But then I remembered Ingrid, my roommate at University of California, Santa Barbara, who grew up in Angola, on the west coast of Africa. One day she was walking her German shepherd through a cashew grove in her backyard. The dog noticed a cobra that was about to strike Ingrid and he jumped in front of her. The snake sprayed venom into the dog's eyes, blinding him, and then the snake bit him. The snake killed Ingrid's German shepherd, but he saved her life.

Pacific rattlesnakes do not have venom as potent as the Angolan cobra, but they feel minute vibrations in the ground to detect the location of their prey. The snake would be able to feel the vibrations from my feet and the paws of three Newfoundland dogs.

Over the years living in Emerald Bay, Brian had only seen a few rattlesnakes, but I considered what I would do if Otis, Pork, or Beans were bitten. How would I carry them to a veterinarian and would the vet have an antidote to the snake venom? I considered how I would walk back to the house with the dogs if one of them was bitten.

Ferruccio, Roberto, and Donatella looked concerned. Ferruccio said there were four types of vipers in Italy. Their venom was not that poisonous to humans, but it might kill a dog. He and his friends were always careful when they walked in the hills or Alps with their dogs.

Worried about the snakes, I decided to turn around and take Otis, Pork, and Beans to the beach. The dogs immediately recognized the direction we were heading. They became as excited as children going to the beach for the day to play. Brian had mentioned they loved the water, but I had no idea how much joy it gave them.

Emerald Bay has a private beach where dogs are allowed to be off leash. I was not sure if they would obey me if I called them, so I had stuffed my pants pockets with huge dog biscuits, their favorite treats, and I had them smell my pockets so they knew the treats were there. I let them off leash and called them back, told them to sit and stay and rewarded them with some pieces of biscuit. They realized they would get more treats if I called them, so I felt confident they would listen to me.

Each beach has its own surf, its own sound. Emerald Bay surf has a rising, rolling, crashing sound. Santa Barbara, California, surf has a sustained crashing sound that echoes like distant thunder. Pemaquid Point in Maine has pounding, clapping surf that explodes and shatters into salty spray.

Otis, Pork, and Beans heard that call and they responded. They were eager to get into the ocean.

Rolling up my pants, I waded knee-deep in the water. The air was filled with the sounds of breaking waves. The cool, salty spray made the air tingle. A dark green line appeared on the surface, and the wave moved from deep to shallow water, growing to a meter and a half. Curling into a perfectly shaped transparent green wave it exploded into white and rushed up the sand. The dogs waded into the water with me. As the waves broke around our legs and the backwash lassoed them, we were pulled deeper into the water. I was getting drenched and so were Otis, Pork, and Beans, but none of us minded.

The wave action was creating small rip currents about ten to twenty meters wide. I was not sure if the dogs were strong swimmers, but if we were caught in a rip, all we needed to do was to swim parallel to the beach for about fifty meters and then into shore. I was confident they would be able to stay with me. They surrounded me and nudged me with their noses deeper into the water.

Carefully, I scanned the ocean for boats, jellyfish, and any debris that might injure the dogs. The coast was clear so I asked them, "Do you want to go for a swim?"

They looked at me like they could not wait to get into the water. I was intrigued and excited. I had seen English pointers and cocker spaniels, Brittany spaniels, Nova Scotia duck tolling retrievers, Irish setters, Portuguese water dogs, and so many other breeds swim, but this was the first time I would see a Newfoundland in the water.

Pulling my long hair back into a ponytail, I returned to the beach, piled my clothes far above the high tide line, adjusted my swimsuit straps, and wrapped my goggles around my wrist. When the dogs saw my swimsuit, they started barking loudly, constantly, and gleefully. Beans was on my heels, and Pork and Otis were bouncing around me. Somehow, they knew that to avoid being hammered by an incoming wave they had to wait until there was a lull in the surf so we could swim beyond the area where it broke.

As we moved into water above our heads, Beans swam near my heels, and Otis and Pork were on either side of me. This configuration reminded me of watching dolphin mothers, who put their young between themselves and another family member to protect them from orcas and sharks. If a shark approached their pod, an adult dolphin swam under the shark and rammed its soft underbelly, trying to burst its spleen, rendering it unconscious or killing it. It was strange; I thought I needed to constantly watch over the three dogs (I did), but I had not realized that they would be watching over me.

Ferruccio said whether the Newfoundlands were in Italy, California, Canada, or anywhere around the globe, they were natural-born lifeguards. It was their nature to watch over people.

I was starting to realize that. Still, I was not sure how far Otis, Pork, and Beans could swim, so I decided to go two hundred meters and see if they could stay with me. I swam dog paddle and they paddled alongside effortlessly. They had an extraordinary feel for the water; their movements were smooth, flowing, and completely efficient, and they knew how to maintain a steady pace.

When we had swum about two hundred meters parallel to shore, I paused and turned toward the dogs to see if they were tired and needed to stop. Otis, Pork, and Beans seemed confused, unsure why I had stopped. They glanced at me and at one another. They were communicating in dog, but I did not know what they were trying to tell me.

Listening to my story, Ferruccio beamed. He knew

exactly what they were telling me—don't stop, just keep swimming.

But I did not know if they could continue. I did not know if they were in shape and did not know how to gauge their endurance. We just kept swimming. And the dogs looked like the happiest hounds. They were grinning, paddling quickly, and bouncing with the waves. I loved it. It was like swimming with my best friends.

A flock of stealthy brown pelicans with wingspans of nearly two meters dropped from the sky and flew so close to our heads that we felt the breeze from their beating wings. And after they passed us, they glided, and their brown wing tips touched the emerald-green water.

Our eyes followed their path across the bay, and when we were almost at the other side, I decided to stretch out my strokes and swim freestyle. Immediately Otis, Pork, and Beans lowered their heads so their chins were almost resting on the water. This lifted their hips, and that made them more streamlined. They swam more efficiently and moved considerably faster. We turned around and swam back across Emerald Bay. All I could think about was how much fun we were having and how I really did not want to stop.

When we reached our starting point outside the wave break, the dogs were not winded, not a bit tired. Like endurance swimmers, they seemed to have warmed up and gained more energy. Otis, Pork, and Beans knew how to pace themselves. They were experts at that. And they absolutely loved to swim. When I asked them again if they wanted to get out, they looked at me as if they were asking me why we would ever want to do that. Then I noticed they were watching the water. There was a dark emerald-green line moving toward us. It was a wave beginning to form. They were waiting. They were perfectly positioned. Otis, Pork, and Beans turned to face shore and put the wave on their backs.

16

Minestrone and Bodysurfing

I stopped my story for a few moments as the server set steaming bowls filled with minestrone alla Milanese in front of each of us. The soup was a garden of vegetables poured into three small bowls. Tender potatoes, carrots, tomatoes, green cabbage, zucchini, onion, celery, green beans, cannellini beans, basil, parsley, rosemary, garlic, and bay leaves were simmered with chicken broth and then pancetta and rice were added. Ferruccio explained this was a favorite northern Italian dish. It was sprinkled with Parmesan cheese, and that saltiness enhanced all the flavors in the soup. After I tasted the first spoonful, I wanted more. The server returned with a small bubbling-hot pizza topped with thinly sliced caramelized pear and gorgonzola cheese.

Ferruccio asked what the Newfoundlands at Emerald Bay had been doing wading in the waves.

I continued. Otis, Pork, and Beans were going body-surfing. I was astonished. I didn't know dogs could do that.

Ferruccio and Roberto and Donatella looked equally incredulous. They also had never heard of dogs being able to bodysurf.

I looked at Otis, Pork, and Beans and saw them sliding toward an incoming wave. It was small and flowed past us. We swam farther out. We felt the tug of a rising wave pulling us toward it. We studied its shape as it began to form a funnel and we gauged how fast it was moving.

This wave was also small and weak, and too little to ride. It slid past us.

Another dark green line expanded across Emerald Bay. It rose into a translucent aqua mound, lifted and dropped us, and slid by. Patiently the dogs floated as if they were resting on surfboards. Their wide and tapered chests were their surfboards. They paddled around and gazed out to sea. They were so at home in the water.

I put on my goggles and looked down through the clear water; I saw a world of fish swimming below us. There were two gray smooth hounds, also known as sand sharks. They swam gracefully at about a leg's distance from us. They were half my size, their bodies elongated and their tails slender. Hovering above the bottom was a guitarfish—a ray with a flat head and trunk. It was hunting for clams, worms, and crabs. There must have been a lot of food in the water. When a slender silvery-bronze leopard shark with dark ovals in neat rows along her back swam under us, I froze and watched her. She was an elegant shark and she swam effortlessly. Smiling to myself, I remembered that leopard sharks were members of the hound shark family. She was probably employing her ampullae of Lorenzini to detect our electromagnetic fields, and I think that Otis, Pork, and Beans felt her. They were paddling closer to me as she swam right below us.

I looked up to get a breath and check the surf.

A large California sea lion was swimming the bay toward a rocky area. The dogs noticed the sea lion and perked their ears. The sea lion looked at them and barked repeatedly. The dogs barked back to communicate in a language shared by the species.

"Here comes a wave!" I shouted.

They felt the energy of the wave before I said it and they had already moved into position. We swam and caught it and rode it only a short way. The energy of the wave dissipated, but I don't think the dogs were disappointed. They quickly turned and swam back out with me beside them. It was so much fun to watch their big heads bob in the water.

There was another long lull, and then a darker green line appeared on the water's surface.

We watched the life around us. Western gulls rose like

smoke above Emerald Bay and circled in the sky. Their loud "keow, keow, keow" calls punctuated the air. California least terns made sharp curves and rapid dives. They were the acrobats of the sky. Great blue herons nesting in nearby eucalyptus trees flew lower to the water. A brown pelican climbed nearly straight up to get a bird's-eye view. When it spotted something in the water, it dove and tucked its wings so they would not break when it hit the water with an explosive impact, catching a fish in its pouch. A flock of black cormorants beating their wings rapidly flew a few meters off the water, and a black skimmer flew with its beak open, scooping fish from the sea.

A wave was moving toward us a lot faster than the ones from before. It was pulling us out toward it. The dogs were watching intensely. They were waiting for that perfect moment when the wave reached its full height, just before it curled. I watched the three Newfoundlands rising higher and higher.

We turned quickly, put the wave on our backs, faced the beach, and sprinted. We were pulling and kicking as fast as we could move our arms and legs. We achieved the speed of the wave and caught it. I looked over. I could not believe I was bodysurfing with three Newfoundlands. We were all having the time of our lives.

Otis, Pork, and Beans were bodysurfing on their stomachs with their front legs stretched out in front of them. They were leaning forward, their heads low and hips high so there would be no drag. They were bodysurfing perfectly, leaning in the direction of the breaking wave and extending their ride.

We were riding a wave—one of nature's most beautiful creations. Completely immersed in the green funnel. We were surrounded by the power and speed of the water. We were one with the wave. We dropped down the face, bounced in bubbly white foam, and spray erupted around us. The wave was losing its strength, weakening, slowing, dissipating, and it seemed like it was dying, but the energy wave that came from the distant storms moved into and through the earth, and what little energy the wave had left delivered us to shallow water. We touched down from our out-of-this-world experience.

It seemed like the sea was celebrating our arrival. Moon snail shells, purple dwarf olive shells, California cone shells, and keystone limpet shells were spinning and fluttering in the water like confetti.

The dogs charged from the water and chased one another on the beach. They ran to me. They were wagging their hips and tails, dancing, shaking, running along the beach, romping in and out of the surf. Happy howling and barking. They were ecstatic. They were high from the thrill of bodysurfing. They were adrenaline hounds.

They looked back at the Pacific Ocean. They heard the call of the waves.

"Do you want to go bodysurfing some more?" I asked.

They barked wildly, pranced, and lifted their muzzles so their voices would rise to the heavens and cross distant seas.

"Let's go," I said.

They loped into the water and charged through the surf. Otis and Pork duck-dived under a breaking wave and popped up on the back side. But Beans dove late, and the wave caught her, flipped her head over tail. I sprinted to the area where I last saw her. She surfaced, but another wave slammed into her and pinned her under. Somehow, she managed to pull herself back to the surface. Worried she was choking, I swam quickly to her. She looked at me. She seemed fine, but I was not sure, so I turned and started to swim toward the beach, hoping that she would follow. She did not. I asked her if she wanted to go back out.

An incoming wave broke. Beans dove under it and cleared the impact zone. She swam out. Being tumbled was part of bodysurfing. She was unfazed and raring to get back out.

Otis and Pork were waiting for us. They were watching small waves slide past. Calm, relaxed, and at one with the ocean, they floated. If they had been human beings, we probably would have talked about the meaning of life, discussed the state of the world, the expanding universe, and maybe talked about Sirius—the Dog Star—the brightest star visible from earth, flickering in a rainbow of colors. But we did not need to speak and we were free floating, and feeling the beating of our hearts, the ease of our breaths, the joy of being alive.

The dogs' ears perked as we looked out across Emerald Bay for the next big wave. I realized they were listening to the distant sound of waves shattering against the rocky headlands. I thought they might be able to judge the size of the waves by these sounds. There were long lulls when the ocean became quiet.

Three weak waves slid by, and then there was another lull.

That space between the waves was like the rests between notes of music or the space between words on a page. In that space between the waves I discovered something new.

While the Pacific Ocean appeared to be calm—*tranquillo*—that calm was only on the surface; it was a crucible of energy and motion. Pulled by the gravitational forces of the moon and the sun, moved by the earth's rotation, the ocean's tides were ebbing and flowing. Energy transmitted by distant storms, strong winds, and calving icebergs was traveling across the ocean. That energy wave would be transformed into a water wave, and that wave would become a sound wave that becomes music. The life, death, and rebirth of a wave I saw and heard as a piece of music.

The energy moving through the water was like a basso continuo—a firm repeating musical bass line. The basso kept building as the wave rushed forward and began to move more freely with a musical accelerando. Racing toward shore the wave crescendoed higher and higher, louder and louder to a fortissimo, its loudest point.

We caught the wave immersed in the music. Dog-paddling as fast as our arms and legs could move, we rode the wave as it lifted us to its climax, and suddenly the wave's strength intensified and it hit the beach with a crashing sforzando. We fell fantastically forward in the green funnel, edged with sunlit silver and white-water lace; we glided into the wave's beautiful cadenza. Otis, Pork, and Beans were leaning into the wave sustaining their speed and fun, riding the music for as long as the watery notes would carry them.

With a twinge of sadness, we heard and felt the decrescendo of the wave as it weakened and grew softer and moved slower in a ritardando. We listened to the wave slide up the beach in a beautiful glissando and then backwash softly to the sea to complete the circle of the piece of music, as the finale of the first musical wave becomes the beginning of another.

Barking joyfully, the dogs shook notes of water from their heads and ears. Pork pushed me with his big black nose. They wanted to go for another ride on a new wave and hear a new song. They wanted to feel the exuberant energy of the wave flow around them. So did I. The dogs multiplied the joy I felt at being alive, being with them, and bodysurfing with them in the ocean.

All afternoon we rode the waves. Pork, Beans, and Otis

never tired. Each wave seemed to give them more energy. Each wave was unique and each ride was different. We kept surfing and swimming and at some time that afternoon we saw a pod of dolphins. I think the dogs heard them first.

The dolphins were emitting high-pitched squeaks, long whistles, trills, and groans. And they were making clicking sounds to echolocate and identify fish in the water. I wondered what they thought of the three Newfoundlands and the sounds we were making as we surfed.

We watched three dolphins ride a wave in synchronization. Their streamlined bodies moved through transparent green water as they bodysurfed below the waves. They looked like gray torpedoes riding the wave toward shore. They used their powerful dolphin kicks to stay inside the wave, but they knew they needed to kick out early and leap over the wave before it collapsed so they would not be tossed ashore and grounded. They were beautiful natural-born bodysurfers.

The only reason we stopped bodysurfing that day was because the wind came up and blew the waves out. We were tired and happy and hungry. It was my first time bodysurfing with Newfoundlands. It would not be my last. We would spend some of the best dog days of summer bodysurfing in Emerald Bay.

17

First Course Home Run

Ferruccio and Roberto and Donatella had never taken their Terranovas bodysurfing, but now they were eager to try it. It would be a new skill the dogs could learn and that would make them more versatile in the water; it would keep them engaged and make them happy hounds.

I asked Ferruccio if he ever experienced dogs that were afraid of water. He said that he did, but it was rare. Most people started their dogs swimming when they were puppies. If the dogs were scared, their owners and instructors worked with them and through time the dogs were able to gain confidence and overcome their fear.

Ferruccio asked if I had any experiences with dogs that were fearful of water.

I told him that there were two dogs and two children that I worked with that were terrified of water.

I took a sip of my drink and started my story about Jimmy. As a young boy, he was terrified of water. He became afraid when his swimming instructor just picked him up and tossed him into the deep end of a pool. He expected Jimmy to swim.

Hearing this, Donatella, Ferruccio, and Roberto looked horrified, and they wondered how someone could be so heartless with a child.

I said that I did not understand either, but this conversation gave me the opportunity to ask them about their dogs. One of the greatest concerns I had when I watched the video of the lifeguard dogs leaping from a helicopter was whether they were forced to jump from the helicopter even if they did not want to. And I wondered if puppies resisted training, were they tossed into the water?

Shocked, Ferruccio said they never threw puppies into the water. They taught puppies the skills and made sure they felt safe. The puppies learned and became confident. Sometimes the older dogs swam with the puppies so they would see how to swim and the puppies would imitate the older dogs.

Equally surprised, Roberto said they never forced a dog to leap out of a helicopter or from a boat. If a dog did not want to jump, they were not forced to do it.

"How old was the boy?" Ferruccio asked.

"Five years old," I said.

Anger and disbelief filled his eyes.

Roberto could not believe people would throw children into the water and expect them to swim.

"Some people believe that if you throw someone in the water their instincts will kick in and they will swim. I think people need to learn to swim the way you teach your dogs," I said.

"Yes, you saw us. We hold them and teach them, and the older dogs, they help teach and coach the puppies. It is fun for them and fun for us," Ferruccio said.

I nodded and told him that I taught private swimming lessons and worked with open-water swimmers and triathletes. They all had fear of the water or things that frightened them about the ocean. Working with Jimmy was one of my biggest challenges. He was so afraid he shook and turned white with fear when he saw me.

For the first few lessons Jimmy's grandmother had to run through the house to catch him and carry him to the pool. He would start screaming, crying, and kicking. His grandmother would hand him to me and hurry into the house. He would be so worked up that he would start coughing, choking, and gasping for air.

The first time we met, he was so afraid that he tried to scratch, hit, and bite me. I held him and spoke calmly, but he continued screaming and started shouting, "No, no, no, I don't want to get in the water. Leave me alone."

I told him he needed to stop crying so he could hear me. Jimmy slapped me across the cheek. I reached for and held his small wrist and told him that it was not okay to hit me. I told him I would never hit him. I promised I would never do anything to hurt him. And I continued to speak slowly and softly so he had to stop screaming so he could hear me.

It was horrible. In my entire life, I had never seen anyone so frightened. I knew this was going to be incredibly difficult for him, and it was going to be extremely challenging for me. I needed to teach him so he would be safe around the water, and I did not want to do anything that would make him even more fearful.

I told him that he needed to learn how to swim so that if anyone pushed him in the water again, he could swim to the side of the pool. He needed to be able to swim so he could survive.

I held him and said I promised he would be okay and we would figure out how to do this together.

I carried Jimmy into the water and told him he could hold on to me or to the side of the pool so he would feel comfortable. He climbed higher in my arms as I stepped down into the water. I wanted him to know that people cared about him. I said that I wanted him to be safe in the water, as did his grandmother and parents.

Jimmy really did not care what anyone else wanted. All he wanted to do was escape. Calmly, I asked him if he could tell me what happened to him.

He said that Bob, the swimming instructor, threw him into the deep end of a pool. He did not know how to swim and sank rapidly to the bottom. Looking up through the water, he could see Bob looking down at him. He could not breathe. He was trying to move his arms to get to the surface, but it didn't work.

Finally, Bob jumped into the pool, grabbed Jimmy, pulled him to the surface, and lifted him out of the pool. He demanded that Jimmy stop crying. He said Jimmy was not trying to learn to swim, so he told him that he better start learning now, and he picked Jimmy up.

Jimmy screamed, "No, no, no, don't throw me in the water. I can't swim."

But Bob ignored him. He dropped Jimmy into the deep end again. Jimmy tried frantically to swim but got a mouthful of water and choked. Jimmy said he felt like he was drowning.

Bob jumped into the pool and dragged Jimmy out. He shouted at Jimmy, telling him again that he was not trying. Jimmy said it was worse the second time because he had asthma and he could not catch his breath.

Now I understood why Jimmy was so afraid. I told him that he had had a very bad teacher, that no one had the right to treat him that way. No one had the right to throw him in the pool. No one had the right to hurt or frighten him. Throwing or pushing someone in a swimming pool is extremely dangerous. He could have been seriously injured. That happened to a daughter of one of my coaches. Kids were playing around the pool and she was pushed into the water. She hit her head on the concrete bottom and was paralyzed for life.

Unfortunately, there are many people who believe that the best way to teach children and adults is to just throw them in the water. There was an Olympic swimming coach from Denmark who taught this way. My friend's daughter Jeanine was so afraid of the coach that she tried to escape by grabbing on to the gutter and climbing out of the pool. But the coach caught her by her feet and pulled her back in. Jeanine hit the side of the pool and knocked out her two front teeth. Because the coach was an Olympic swimmer, Jeanine's parents accepted this as the best way to teach their child. I wished Jeanine had never had this bad experience because she had to overcome so much fear before she eventually learned to swim from a different instructor.

I needed to ensure that Jimmy understood that my teaching methods were different.

I told Jimmy that the best swimming instructors were gentle, caring, encouraging, and supportive. I asked him if he was learning to read. He said he was. I told him that learning to swim was just like learning to read. When he was learning to read, he learned one word and then another and eventually he could read a sentence and an entire book. He could go to a library and find amazing books and read great stories or he could buy books at bookstores and online and learn about himself, his dogs, the world, and beyond, even the universe. Just like a beginning reader, he would learn one swimming skill, then he would learn another, building upon what he learned each step of the way. Eventually he would be able to pull his hand and then the other and kick and swim across the pool.

Jimmy was starting to focus his eyes on me. The most important part of swimming is being able to breathe. If he could not breathe, he could not relax and he could not swim. When he breathed his lungs filled up like two balloons and that helped him float.

Jimmy was listening, so I told him this was the way I was taught to swim and the way I would teach him. Once I learned the swimming basics from my parents, they took me to the YWCA and I learned all four swimming strokes: butterfly, backstroke, breaststroke, and freestyle. The swimming instructors were great and I discovered that I loved swimming. They encouraged me to join the Manchester, New Hampshire, swim team. When I was twelve years old, my parents moved our family to California so I could train with an Olympic coach. In high school I swam on both the girls' and boys' swim teams and played on the boys' water polo team—there was no girls' team at the time—and competed on a club water polo team. I swam and played water polo at the University of California, Santa Barbara, and was an assistant coach for both the men's swim and water polo teams. During university I took Red Cross classes in water safety and swimming instruction to be able to teach swimming. I also earned my lifeguard qualification and became a lifeguard. I had my CPR and advanced first aid certifications. Working with friends who taught at the YMCA and the Jewish Community Center, I improved my teaching techniques. I gave private swimming lessons to children, adults, and dogs. I swam with Olympic swimmers and Olympic coaches and then for many years I coached triathletes and open-water swimmers who wanted to learn how to swim in the ocean and swim faster. Some of them were frightened of swimming in the ocean, but I had a lot of experience. I had broken many world records for swimming in the open water.

Jimmy understood that I had been teaching for a long time and that my method was different from what he had experienced. But the only thing that really caught his attention was that I taught dogs how to swim. He was surprised that dogs needed to learn to swim. I said just like people, some dogs instinctively knew what to do when they were put in the water, but other dogs needed to learn what to do.

Jimmy started to relax and breathe. His body became less rigid. His fear was so strange, as one of the things that I most loved in life was being in the water. It made me feel alive and elated, and swimming gave me some of my greatest and lasting friendships. But for Jimmy the water was the thing he hated and feared the most. Getting into a pool was reliving his nightmare. He thought he would drown. With patience, trust, understanding, and love I knew we would transform Jimmy's deep fear of the water into fascination.

We had a long way to go, but this traumatic event had happened just recently, two or three weeks earlier. The sooner we could change the way Jimmy felt about the water, the sooner he would be able to focus on learning to swim and enjoying being in the water.

I asked Jimmy if he could hold my hand so we could climb into the pool together. He nodded tentatively.

Clenching my hand so tightly it turned white, in a shaky voice he said he thought he would be okay. Walking stiffly, he forced himself to the pool's edge and stood staring at the water for at least thirty seconds, trying to build up his courage. I told him we could hold hands and get into the water together and I would continue to hold his hand for as long as he wanted.

He looked at me and inched forward. It was torture. He was shaking and squeezing his eyes closed like he was in excruciating pain. I encouraged him.

He took the first step, and quickly the second step, and suddenly he felt the water creeping up to his waist.

Assuring him that I would not let go of his hand, I asked him, "You play baseball, right?"

He nodded and smiled slightly.

"We're on second. Can we try for third base?"

He smiled. "Third step, right?"

"Yes," I said.

Taking a deep breath as if it might be his last, he stepped down and landed safely on the third step. He caught his breath and stepped onto the pool bottom.

"Home run!" I said and swept him up in my arms. I hugged him tightly and told him that he had done a fantastic job. He beamed. Those four steps down would change his life forever.

"Now what are we going to do?" he said, worried, but finding his balance and some more courage.

"Can you let go of my hand for a moment so you can turn around?" I asked.

He tentatively released my hand and slowly turned.

"Look how far you have come. Those were four giant steps. You are very brave. You can smile now," I said.

He grinned. Light came back into his brown eyes and he had started to gain some confidence.

I told him that what I would like to do was walk around the shallow end with him so he could feel the water. I asked him if he wanted to hold my hand or walk on his own. I think he was starting to trust himself more and more. He knew what he was going to do next. He was not sure what I would do. I was not sure either. I had to watch him, make sure he felt safe, show him how he

Dr. Carlo Morlacchi giving Al her first examination. All dogs must have completed their first vaccination cycle and have a good-health certification before they can enter the school.

Twenty Newfoundland dogs from the SICS training on land together with Donatella. They are preparing for the international water rescue meeting with Newfoundlands from Switzerland, France, and Germany.

Zac and Donatella in the Italian Air Force helicopter. They are training with the search and rescue department of Milano for land search and rescue.

Off Genoa in the Ligurian Sea, three people needed to be rescued. Zac followed his crew member and jumped in to rescue them. Zac was known as a force of nature. The Italian saying "Give me a rope and I'll move the world" applied to Zac. Alberto Castelnuovo supervised the rescue.

Donatella with three-month-old Al and Zac the Leonberger. They are on a walk strolling in Brussels along with Al's mom, Al's dad, and his two brothers.

Al and Donatella completing helicopter training in the Maggiore area. This was Al's first flight. She did great.

Donatella and Al are in Cervia, training with the fifteenth Italian Air Force wing. The team was impressed with Al.

Al and Donatella training at the Airgreen helicopter base for the Italian rescue system in Robassomero (Turin), maintaining the skill level required to be part of helicopter rescues.

Al and Donatella on the River Po in Turin are providing assistance to a stand-up paddleboard race, making sure the racers are safe in collaboration with the municipal police of Turin and the dog department unit.

Al and the municipal police watching over the stand-up paddleboarders in Turin.

During the summer Donatella and Al patrol on boats with the Italian Coast Guard around Lake Maggiore.

On board the *Luca Zioni*, patrolling the Gulf of Salò on Lake Garda in the summer.

Al and Gigi Lazzarini always make time to train the younger dogs and the young dogs love it.

To simulate a man-overboard scenario, Donatella sent Al from the Italian Navy ship *Palinuro* to jump into the water and "rescue" sailors from the *Palischermo*, a rowboat crewed by eight sailors and an officer.

At the dock in Milano, Al and Donatella provide lifeguard services for the stand-up paddleboards and dragon boats. Al rides in the bow of a dragon boat with her SICS crew, watching the racers.

On Lake Maggiore, Donatella and Al train with the Port Authority Coast Guard to improve their water-entry techniques and teamwork with the crew.

Al's first experience with stationary and landing helicopters, giving her the chance to become accustomed to the noise and wind created by the helicopter blades. Al was immediately at ease and was eager to board the helicopter.

Continuous training with the Search and Rescue Department of the Italian Air Force maintains the dog unit's high standards of professionalism. They were working together to lower the dog in the winch.

Al and Donatella and members of the SICS are happily welcomed to train in European countries. Here at Lake Lugano, Switzerland, the recovery of a castaway is conducted in coordination with the Swiss civil protection unit.

In winter Al and other dogs with the SICS train at an indoor swimming pool at the Paladog sports center in Cologno Monzese. This is essential to keep the dogs and handlers in training. Al is providing a life buoy to a stranger.

Moments after reaching land after a winch descent from a helicopter, Donatella and Al celebrate an excellent exercise with the Italian Air Force.

could progress, and encourage him, but stop if it was too much for him, if he felt afraid. Otherwise, the gains we made could be lost.

But Jimmy showed me his courage. He said he could walk around the shallow end on his own. I think I saw a shiver race up his back, but he lifted his arms and shook them as if he was trying to shake off his fear. I asked him to feel the water pressing around him, to feel how different it was to walk through the water than it was to walk on land. And to feel how his arms floated and his legs moved slower against the water's resistance. And how the water canceled out some of earth's gravity, so walking through the water was like being an astronaut walking on the moon.

When we were done with the first lesson Jimmy could not believe that was all we were doing that day, so I reminded him of what he had accomplished. He had gotten into the water almost on his own, he had learned how to find his balance, and we had walked across the moon together. But now he had to hurry up and get out of the pool because I had to leave to teach another lesson.

He looked at me with incredible surprise. No one had ever had to tell him to get out of the pool. People spent all their energy trying to convince him to get in.

Quickly, I wrapped Jimmy up in a warm towel and we exchanged high fives. He had done a great job. His smile was as bright as the morning sun. But when I told him that I looked forward to seeing him the next day, his smile faded and his body tensed.

I told him that we were going to have more time to play in the water. We would moonwalk. I promised him that I would never scare him or hurt him and we would always have fun. From his expression, I could tell that someone had not been honest with him. He was not sure I would keep my word. My challenge was to figure out how to make him feel safer in the water, help him overcome his horrible experiences, and motivate him.

The next day the answer came to me when I was whacked by a tail.

18

Primi Piatti—Labrador Water Polo

The owner of the restaurant appeared with three platters—one with cotoletta alla Valdostana, a veal chop stuffed with fontina cheese and prosciutto; another with Umbrian-style chicken alla cacciatora, chicken with lemon, vinegar, olives, capers, rosemary, sage, garlic, and white wine. The third dish was eggplant involtini, a classic vegetarian dish. Roasted slices of eggplant were rolled around a delicious filling of mozzarella and Pecorino Romano cheese, toasted pine nuts, golden raisins, Italian parsley, and bread crumbs. The stuffed eggplant was slowly cooked in a red sauce made with tomatoes, onion, olive oil, lots of garlic, red wine, smoked Spanish paprika, and the zest of an orange. It was light and full of flavor. The food was a feast for the eyes as well as for the stomach.

I continued the story. The next day, Jimmy was in the living room lying on the couch wearing his swimsuit watching cartoons, with his two Labrador retrievers lying down on either side of him. When the dogs heard me enter the room, they ran to me with tails wagging. Jimmy took a couple of steps back when he saw me. Sensing his distrust, the dogs wiggled between him and me, and one dog whacked me with her tail. I told Jimmy that he had two lovely Labradors and that I had a yellow Labrador named Cody. He was my best friend. I asked if we could sit down on the couch together and if he would introduce me to his dogs. Jimmy introduced Juliette and Fifi. He said that Juliette was five years old and Fifi, her daughter, was two years old. Each day for them was a grand adventure, and all they wanted to do was play with Jimmy.

"Do Juliette and Fifi like to play in the water?" I asked Jimmy.

"They love being in the pool," he said.

I was careful not to use the "s" word ("swim") with Jimmy. Instead, I substituted the word "play."

"Do you think they would like to join us?" I asked.

"Sure," Jimmy said with a smile, and when I showed him a handful of coins, his smile grew bigger and he asked what we were going to do with them. I promised I would show him, but I wanted to know if he needed help getting into the water or if he could climb in by himself.

He held my hand and we walked outside to the pool.

I climbed down the steps into the pool. I put a coin on the first step, took a breath, opened my eyes, leaned into the water, picked up the coin, and stood.

Jimmy climbed into the water beside me and eagerly tried to do the same, but he kept floating to the surface. I told him he needed to blow out some bubbles so he could lower himself in the water. He was learning that he could float, and that by regulating his breath he could go under the water and then rise back to the surface. While I held him on his back, his feet came up, and he opened his eyes and breathed. He was floating—he felt it was magical. And for a moment he was not afraid.

Jimmy did not like getting water in his ears, so I told him that that was just part of swimming, that happened to the dogs too and they shook the water out of their ears after they swam. He could get the water out by tipping his head to each side. I asked Jimmy if he was ready for Juliette and Fifi to play with us in the pool. I noticed a tennis ball lying beside the pool and tossed it into the deep end.

Juliette and Fifi launched themselves from the pool's edge. They flew over our heads. They dog-paddled through the air and looked goofy. Juliette belly flopped. Fifi tackled her and tried to tear the tennis ball from Juliette's mouth.

Jimmy laughed so hard he doubled over.

I asked Jimmy to watch how the dogs swam and if he could try to imitate them. The dogs saw him and swam back. I held Jimmy from behind and without any hesitation he was able to dog-paddle for the first time. I told him he was doing great and asked if he could stop and give each dog a hug so they would know that he was okay and that he loved them. Jimmy gave them long hugs and when he climbed out of the water, they jumped up and licked him all over his face.

In a few lessons, Jimmy was diving for coins, floating, and dog-paddling, but he was terrified of swimming in the deep end. I decided to try to change his focus and asked if he would mind if Juliette and Fifi stayed with us for the entire lesson. I asked Jimmy to throw the ball into the middle of the pool while I held Juliette and Fifi by their collars. He threw the ball and I told him to sprint for it and get it before Juliette and Fifi beat him to it. I would give him a three-second lead. Jimmy was competitive, and he dog-paddled as fast as he could go. I shouted out, "One, two, three!" and released the dogs.

They chased him. And I told Jimmy they were gaining on him. They were right on his heels. He reached the ball first, grabbed it, and held it up above his head. Fifi tried to jump up and steal it, but Juliette moved between her and Jimmy and protected him and the ball. I told him he was playing Labrador water polo. He loved it, and from that day on, he could not wait to get into the water. The dogs made all the difference in teaching him to swim. And during each lesson they raced him, helped him build his speed and endurance, and helped him develop his skills playing Labrador water polo. Juliette and Fifi inspired Jimmy to find his courage.

Jimmy mastered all four swimming strokes, learned basic lifesaving, and became a stronger swimmer. Because of his experience playing Labrador water polo he made it onto the Los Alamitos High School water polo team, one of the top teams in Southern California. Juliette and Fifi lived long, happy lives, which were always happier when Jimmy returned home after school and for college breaks. Jimmy grew up to become a businessman and he never lost his love of swimming or dogs. He rescued dogs from shelters and they have become part of his family.

19

Basset Hounds and Puccini

We took a break from talking and eating for a moment, and I noticed music coming from speakers positioned around the patio.

"Is that Puccini?" I asked.

Roberto nodded and smiled. "The owner of the trattoria loves music and dogs. This is from *La Bohème*. It's the café scene when Musetta, one of the main characters in the opera, is singing with her dog," he said.

A man in a stylish black suit and blue silk tie—the owner of the restaurant—came outside to check on us. He wanted to make sure that we were enjoying everything.

We assured him that we were.

I asked him about the Puccini opera. He said it was

a big deal for dogs to be in *La Bohème*. They auditioned for the role. There were all types of terriers, Pomeranians, Tibetan spaniels, French bulldogs, and many other breeds that played the role of Musetta's dog. It was an enormous honor to get the part. The dog had to have something special—an ability to both play the role and to connect with the audience.

We enjoyed listening to the opera for a few minutes and then I told them about Sarah and the basset hounds.

When I first gave Sarah a swimming lesson her grandmother Emily met me by the pool gate, unlocked it, and invited me into the pool area. She apologized for two howling basset hounds, and she introduced me to seven-year-old Sarah, who was standing slightly behind her wearing a light pink swimsuit. Her long blond hair was pulled back into a ponytail and she was speaking at hyperspeed, breathing rapidly, telling me that she was ready to get into the pool. But her hands were shaking. Her grandmother left us so I could work with Sarah. She told her grandmother she would be okay.

We stepped into the warm pool, but Sarah's teeth were chattering. Something was wrong. I asked her if she was cold, she said no, and her blue eyes filled with tears. She blinked them back. Stuttering, she said that she was not cold. Something had happened that made her so afraid. I needed to find out what it was.

"Let's climb out of the pool and talk," I suggested.

"I'm okay now," Sarah protested. She thought I was upset with her.

"Let's talk for a few minutes," I said in a soothing voice.

We sat on the pool's edge and she inhaled sharply.

"Did something bad happen to you when you were in the water?" I asked.

She shook her head and winced. "No. Something happened to our basset hounds. They almost died."

In a soft voice she recounted the story. Her grandparents had two basset hounds, Winnie and Pooh. Winnie was seven years old, like Sarah, and Pooh was five years old. Their fur was short and they got cold easily. They liked to sun themselves on the pool deck, especially during the cool California winters.

Rolling on their backs they let the sun warm their chests and bellies. Even though they looked like they were sleeping they were awake and listening to the sounds around the house. When they heard dogs, cats, coyotes, and squirrels beyond the backyard, they ran to the fence, squeezed their noses under it, and barked. Their loud, deep-throated howls carried throughout the neighborhood.

One morning when Sarah was visiting her grandparents, Winnie was sunbathing by the pool. Sarah was helping her grandfather Joseph trim an orange tree in the backyard while her grandmother was inside. Winnie heard something and jumped to his feet. He alerted Pooh and they raced across the pool deck, but Winnie cut the corner too close and splashed into the water.

Winnie did not know how to swim. His owners had tried to teach him, but his legs were very short and his bones extremely heavy. He could not float. He sank to the bottom of the pool. Sarah saw it happen. She saw him looking up at her with his sad eyes. There was nothing she could do. She did not know how to swim.

Joseph dropped the trimmer and jumped into the pool fully clothed. He dove under the water and tried to grab and lift Winnie, but the dog was too heavy. Joseph had to return to the surface, take a deep breath, and try again. He managed to pull Winnie to the shallow end, but the dog seemed lifeless. Joseph shouted for Sarah to get her grandmother.

Sarah ran into the house yelling for her grandmother. She finally found her in the garage. Emily ran out to the pool and jumped in fully clothed. She didn't pause to kick off her shoes. Together, Joseph and Emily lifted Winnie out of the water.

Water was draining from Winnie's mouth and nose. His eyes were shut. Joseph held the back of his hand up to Winnie's nose to feel for his breath and watched Winnie's chest to see if it was rising and falling. He could not feel Winnie's breath. He opened Winnie's mouth, pulled his tongue forward, and let more water drain from his mouth.

Once the water stopped flowing, Joseph gave Winnie mouth-to-mouth resuscitation. He placed his hand over the dog's muzzle to make sure it was completely closed.

He put his mouth over Winnie's nostrils, blew gently, and watched for his chest to lift and expand. It rose. He removed his mouth from Winnie's nose and muzzle and allowed the air to flow out. Sarah could not remember how many times Joseph repeated the maneuver, but finally Winnie started breathing on his own.

Winnie opened his eyes, but he looked awful. Sarah's grandparents were afraid that he would develop pneumonia or water intoxication from inhaling and ingesting too much water, so they drove him to his veterinarian.

The vet examined Winnie and said he was lucky to be alive, and that Sarah's grandparents were wise to have given him artificial resuscitation. Winnie survived because of their quick actions. The veterinarian prescribed antibiotics to prevent a bacterial infection. Winnie was not himself for a couple of weeks, but he recovered.

Sarah's grandparents never expected an accident would happen again, but a few months later, Winnie and Pooh were chasing a squirrel around the backyard and Pooh fell into the pool. Just like Winnie had before, he immediately sank to the bottom.

Sarah found him and called for her grandparents. They both jumped into the water and pulled poor Pooh out of the pool. The dog wasn't breathing. Joseph ran his hand along the inside of Pooh's hind leg where it met his body and pressed down gently with his fingers to feel for a pulse. Pooh was underwater longer than Winnie had been, and

Joseph was worried his heart might have stopped. He thought he might have to perform CPR on Pooh, but he was able to feel Pooh's pulse and he gave Pooh artificial resuscitation instead.

Sarah said this happened when she was five years old and it scared her to see Winnie and Pooh nearly drown. Because of that she was afraid of the water.

I said she was brave to take swimming lessons. Because of her quick response, her sweet basset hounds survived. She was able to help when it was most needed.

For the first time Sarah realized she had made a great difference in saving Winnie and Pooh from drowning. The dogs had always been a part of her life. They were her best friends. She told me she had nightmares that the dogs fell in the pool again and there was no one there to save them.

In my experience, sometimes the best way to overcome fear is to help someone who is afraid. The best way to make sure Winnie and Pooh were safe around the pool was to teach them to swim and not let them in the pool area unless someone was watching. I asked Sarah if she could help me teach Winnie and Pooh to swim.

Sarah agreed to help me.

My concern, though, was if Winnie and Pooh were afraid they would bite, as dogs sometimes become aggressive when they are frightened.

Sarah's grandmother said Winnie and Pooh had never

bitten anyone. Even when Sarah was a toddler and she bumped them when they were sleeping and startled them, they never snapped. Sometimes when they were sleeping, Sarah rested her head on one of them and they slept beside her. They loved having her close.

Still, I could not be sure that we could do this safely. I decided that I would hold the dogs' chests up and keep their heads above the water and have Sarah stand behind me and hold their tails. Before we had a dog climb into the water with us, I would show Sarah the new skills we wanted to teach them, such as pulling and kicking.

Winnie looked like he was in shock when Sarah's grandmother handed him to me in the pool. It seemed like he could not believe that we were putting him in the water. It felt like he tightened every muscle in his body, and in that state he would sink.

I spoke to him calmly, hoping that he would relax, and I told Sarah how to move her hands and arms in the water so she could demonstrate the dog paddle for him. I moved his paws in the same paddling motion. He was frozen with fear. When it was his turn, Pooh reacted the same way, but Sarah and I continued working with them. Winnie and Pooh learned to swim, but their bodies were so heavy they could only stay up for about ten seconds. That wasn't long enough for them to survive, so the grandparents got them life jackets and would not let the dogs in the pool area unless they were wearing them and supervised.

Sarah learned to swim all four strokes and she liked the water. She grew up to be tall, graceful, flexible, and exceedingly coordinated. She became a dancer, and whenever she faced a challenge in dancing or in her life in general, she remembered how she decided to be brave and master something she was afraid of. She was proud that she had helped Winnie and Pooh learn to swim.

Ferruccio and Roberto were not surprised. They said some dogs do not float well in the water because of their body types and they fight the water to keep their heads up.

It is the same for people who are lean, who feel like they cannot float and struggle in the water. They can float, but they float at a lower level than someone with more body fat.

I told Ferruccio and Roberto and Donatella that I heard there were other dog breeds that were not designed for swimming. A friend's bulldog fell in the backyard pool and before he could be saved, he sank to the bottom and drowned. It was heartbreaking.

"Dogs swim in circles when they are disoriented," Donatella said. She saw this happen with dogs they trained at the school. When they were in the lakes and in the sea, they knew where to get in and out of the water. They could see the shore. But when they were invited to train in a local swimming pool, they became confused. From their perspective, everything in the pool was flat. Everything looked the same. They did not have landmarks to see where to climb out. They became disoriented and swam erratically and in circles. If they choked on water they started to panic, but they were wearing swim vests and they did not sink. Their owners guided them to the pool steps so they would learn to climb out. Some dogs managed to use the steps, while other dogs never learned.

This helped me understand what had happened to our family dogs. We had three Italian greyhounds. They were delicate dogs, lean and streamlined—like toy greyhounds. The breed was known as the "lap dog of royalty." Frederick the Great, Anne of Denmark, Queen Victoria, and King James I had Italian greyhounds. Catherine the Great, empress of Russia, also loved the breed. Her favorite was Zemira, a delicate grey named for an opera character. The breed was popular around the globe.

We named the mother Gazelle because she looked like that beautiful animal, and her puppies were named Mighty Mouse, because she lifted and carried items that looked like they were twice her weight, and Bruno, because he was tall and handsome. Roberto and Ferruccio smiled when they heard the names. They thought they fit the dogs—a lot better than Pork and Beans.

They were much different from the poodles, beagles, and other dogs we had when I was young. The Italian greyhounds were elegant sight hounds with long, graceful lines and curved backs. They were playful, affectionate, and incredibly swift on land, but they were terrible swimmers. Like Winnie and Pooh, Bruno, Mighty Mouse, and Gazelle loved to race around the backyard pool and circle it as if they were on a racetrack. Sometimes they tumbled into the water. They were extremely negatively buoyant.

For a few moments they could frantically dog-paddle and keep their heads above the water, but their long, thin legs and small paws were ineffective. The weight of their muscular bodies made them sink. Sometimes they reached the side of the pool and clung to it, but they could only hold on for a few seconds.

Because my parents were so safety-oriented, they always watched the pool when children and dogs were in the backyard. They never left any of us unsupervised. But I have an adult friend who had a German shepherd. She went to work one morning and when she returned home at the end of the day, she discovered her German shepherd had drowned in her pool. Another friend lost her pug in the pool.

Roberto said that people who had dogs with stubby legs and long bodies like dachshunds, corgis, and Dandie Dinmont terriers had to be particularly careful with their dogs around water because they were not good swimmers.

Roberto said there were special swim vests designed for dogs to help them keep their heads above water. The vests were used at the school to help the dogs float and stay high in the water so they could rescue people. Owners could have their dogs wear these swim vests if they had a pool or if they were doing water sports and wanted to take their dog with them. People still needed to watch their dog just like they must watch a child or adult when near or in the water.

Making sure people and dogs were safe in and around the water was Ferruccio's life's work.

"Every adventure, every training exercise, every trip, every rescue stays in my heart," Ferruccio said and smiled slowly, realizing the key to why he loved doing it so much.

And he did this with his best friends, Roberto and Donatella, who had been at the core of the Scuola Italiana Cani Salvataggio for almost as many years as he had.

Roberto told me that during the summer months certified water rescue dogs and their owners are stationed at forty-eight beaches and lakes in Italy. They patrol with the Guardia Costiera. They have prevented hundreds of drownings. There are about three hundred certified water rescue dogs in Italy. Ferruccio said he had also taught dogs in Germany and Switzerland to become water rescue dogs.

Roberto told me that in the morning Al and Donatella were joining the Guardia Costiera and they invited me to sail with them.

I glanced at Donatella and realized why she looked so tense and was so quiet during dinner.

Al was having a test in the morning with the Guardia Costiera crew.

For years Donatella had worked with Al to prepare

her for this. It would be more than just disappointing if she failed. She had always been a different dog and a big challenge.

Donatella was worried her Newfoundland would fail the test.

She left for a moment to make a call.

I turned to Ferruccio and said, "I know Donatella is worried. Do you think it would be better if I decline the invitation to join her for the test tomorrow? I really want to go, but I do not want to be a distraction to Al."

"No, she wants you to see how we train with the Guardia Costiera. Al needs to be able to perform in any situation," Ferruccio said.

It had been a long, perfect day, filled with new adventures, new friends (with and without fur), and delicious food. I could not wait for the morning, but I was also worried. I didn't know what I had done to distract Al. Whatever it was, I didn't want to repeat it and cause her to fail her test. That would be a disaster.

20

Pesto and a Doge's Palace

The drive from Donatella's home near Milan to Genoa would take about two hours. We would be meeting with Admiral Angrisano, commander of the Guardia Costiera, and his crew. Bob, whom I had met during water training, had a sport utility vehicle large enough to comfortably carry Al, Donatella, and me. Donatella sat beside Bob so they could talk about Al's upcoming test. Although I couldn't speak Italian, I could tell that Donatella was asking Bob many questions. Bob answered her in a bright, soothing voice as Al dozed in the back in her secured crate.

We drove on the Autostrada A7, a highway that connects Milan with Genoa. Italian drivers drive fast and pay full attention to the road. We passed trucks, tankers, and compact cars and flashed past fields that framed the highway. Some fields were filled with vibrant green rice paddies.

Donatella explained that Italian farmers were growing new coveted hybrid rice. For centuries the Chinese had grown black rice, known as "forbidden rice." It was rare and only served to emperors and their families. There were attempts to plant the forbidden rice in northern Italy. It couldn't endure the cold winters, but recently a rice hybridizer successfully crossed forbidden rice with a local northern Italian variety. The new whole-grain rice known as "*Venere nero*"—black Venus rice—is valued for its nutty flavor and sweetness and has four times more iron than white rice and contains high levels of antioxidants; its hull has minerals like magnesium, manganese, and phosphorus. *Venere nero* was a new health food, more expensive than common rice, but it was delicious, especially when served with seafood. I hoped all the conversation about food was helping to distract Donatella from worrying about the test.

As we approached Genoa, a city that lies between the Ligurian Sea and the Apennine Mountains and spreads out along the coast for about thirty kilometers, we drove through a series of long tunnels and onto an elevated highway that wove through the city, giving us glimpses of modern buildings, offices, and tall apartments.

We parked and collected Al from the back of the SUV.

She leaped out, ready to go. I think she felt Donatella's
tension, as she kept looking up at her with her large gold
eyes. She walked right beside her as Donatella led the way
through a maze of cobblestone streets, across paved bou-
levards, and along winding alleys.

The city was vibrant, even though it was early in the
morning. People were walking the streets in business and
casual clothes. Cyclists, motorcyclists, vans, and small
trucks were navigating the narrow streets and the air was
filled with sounds of vehicles, voices of people speaking
Italian, and construction workers shouting over the din of
jackhammers. I caught glimpses of people standing outside chatting, sitting at cafés drinking espresso and eating
cornetto—small Italian croissants—reading the newspa-
per, hanging out laundry from apartments overhead. The
sound of bells rang from churches near and far.

A handsome young man in his thirties walked across
the street. He looked like he was on the way to work. He
was wearing a tailored navy-blue suit and seemed to be
in a hurry, but he suddenly noticed a beautiful woman
with long black hair and sunglasses, wearing a flowing
summer dress that was turquoise, yellow, white, and navy.
The navy blue in her dress matched the man's suit. Rec-
ognizing each other, they smiled, and the young man ran
to her. So caught up in their embrace, the couple was
unaware of anything else in the world. People were stopping, watching, smiling with delight. Love was in the air.

I was in Italy.

We continued our walk and I saw ancient buildings, plazas with fountains, and cathedrals. Genoa was Columbus's hometown. There was a woman and a little boy looking at a monument celebrating Columbus. I wondered what she was saying to her son. Was she encouraging him to become a great explorer, to sail across great oceans? Was she telling him that he needed to sail beyond the bonds of what he knew and discover new things—things that would enrich his life and the people his life touched? The little boy was completely focused on what his mother was saying, until he saw pigeons land and stop to drink some water caught in the cracks between the stones.

A cyclist came close to the pigeons. They lifted off in a wave of wings. Al saw them and charged. Donatella told her to stop. She wouldn't listen. Al was towing Donatella as she chased them. She yelled at her in a sharp tone and finally got her to stop. Al was so headstrong, I wondered if Donatella would be able to control her during the test.

We continued our walk and it felt like this was the natural rhythm of Genoa, a typical day in a coastal city. But there was nothing typical about this day for Donatella. The lines in the corners of her eyes looked even more tense.

Suddenly we got a whiff of warm baked bread and I saw a sign for a *fornaio*—bakery.

Al lifted her big brown head, sniffed, and tasted the air.

Her mouth started watering. Glancing at Donatella, she picked up her pace.

At the bakery's front door, Al barked deep, loud barks until a middle-aged man with black hair and brown eyes, wearing an apron smudged with flour, greeted us warmly. He scratched Al's head and she looked up at the baker with drool and adoration.

Speaking to Al in Italian, he told her that he was happy to have her visit and that she was a good girl. He asked Donatella if he could give her a small piece of focaccia.

Al took the bread from the baker's large muscular hands, carefully making sure not to bite, and wagged her tail.

Donatella knew that our walk to the Guardia Costiera would be slow and that we would be stopping frequently. A tiny woman with a curved back, probably in her eighties, was sweeping the sidewalk in front of her apartment. She stopped when she saw Al. She held the dog's massive head in her tiny hands and told Al she was a beautiful girl. A woman riding a bicycle stopped momentarily to ask about Al. Three teenage boys who turned a corner asked if she was a Terranova. They asked if she was one of the lifeguard dogs.

Donatella said she was training to be one.

They thought that was awesome.

People in Genoa and all over Italy and Europe recognized the water rescue dogs from the Scuola Italiana Cani

Salvataggio. They knew that the dogs worked with the Guardia Costiera and the dogs helped to save eight to ten people a year. They prevented hundreds of drownings by intervening before someone needed to be rescued.

People came out of their shops when they saw Al walking by. She took up half the sidewalk and was hard to miss. A woman with her grandson asked if he could pet Al.

Lowering her head, Al looked the child in the eye, and the small boy gently petted her. He wrapped his arm around Al's back and she swished her tail quickly so he could hear her happiness.

We had half an hour before our meeting, so Donatella and Bob offered to take me on a short walking tour of Genoa. It was good for Al to walk off some stress, they said, and I think this was what Donatella was trying to do too.

We passed by the Palazzo Ducale. A young woman was sitting on a chair sketching a picture of the Venetian gothic building. Donatella said that it was called the Doge's Palace. I heard her say "dog's palace."

Donatella explained that the Doge's Palace was built in the thirteenth century. The building had served as the seat of the Genoan government and today it housed several museums. All year long there were art shows and cultural events in the palace.

The day was growing warm and it was a relief when we reached Piazza De Ferrari. A massive silver fountain shaped like a spineless sea urchin was filled with flowing water. The soothing sound dampened the roar of nearby traffic and a cool mist sprinkled our faces. Al was roasting in her thick brown coat. She sighed with relief when the spray hit her face. She decided the fountain was a perfect place to cool off. All she needed to do was to climb over the lip at the base. Dogs are not allowed in the fountains in Italy, but she did not read signs.

Taking a few powerful steps, Al was preparing to leap into the fountain. Donatella anticipated Al's next move, tightened her grip on the leash, and ordered her to stop before she broke the law. She stopped but continued to pull hard on the leash and resist Donatella. This was not good. If she could not control Al now, I wondered if she would listen to her when we were on the boat.

We continued our walk past the intersection of the old town of Genoa and the modern financial part of the city, through a maze of narrow alleyways somewhere near Via Garibaldi. We passed baroque palaces and San Lorenzo Cathedral and reached a gate at the Guardia Costiera building. A guard checked our names and invited us in and offered us seats. He said Admiral Angrisano would be with us soon.

Donatella sat for a few moments, handed Al's leash to Bob, and stood up and paced. She was trying to walk off her nervousness and I think she was trying to put a distance between herself and Al so the dog would not be nervous. It seemed to be working. Al was sprawled out on the floor with her head resting on her paws and eyes shut, but her ears were moving in the direction of Donatella's footsteps.

Admiral Angrisano greeted us warmly. He was a medium-sized man, strong, vital, with dark brown eyes and silvering hair. He looked distinguished in his Guardia Costiera uniform. Striding quickly across the room, like he was racing from one meeting to another, Admiral Angrisano immediately shook our hands. When Al saw him, she jumped up and wagged her tail. From the expression on the admiral's face, the way he looked directly at Al with a soft smile, it was clear that he was a dog person, and just being near her was bringing the admiral's blood pressure down. Al leaned toward him and he rubbed her head. She looked blissful.

Admiral Angrisano spoke English fluently. He said he had read about my swimming career and he was impressed. I told him that through the years I had received a lot of help from people, including the United States Coast Guard. When I needed to find out information about a waterway and find boat support, they had pointed me in the right direction. I had friends in the U.S. Coast Guard, some who worked with K-9s, and I was thrilled to meet him and his crew and have the opportunity to go on patrol with them.

He said that they loved working with the water rescue

dogs, that the dogs make people happy. He was smiling as he said it gave the Guardia Costiera a friendly face. But the dogs were far more than mascots; they were directly involved in rescuing people. He was impressed with all the water rescue dogs and proud to be working with them. During one training exercise he said he saw a Newfoundland pull in six people at one time.

He added that the water rescue dogs were trained to watch for someone raising their arms in the water. That was their signal that the person was in distress, and the dogs would react to that cue.

The admiral gave me background about the area. He said that the old harbor, Porto Antico, had been beautifully redesigned and restored by modern architect Renzo Piano. His name was familiar as he was the architect for the New York Times Building.

Quickly he told me about the importance of Genoa. It was the second largest seaport in Italy and one of the largest harbors in Europe. The Guardia Costiera were active in the port. They were involved with search and rescue and boating safety, served as maritime police, investigated maritime accidents, and had many more tasks. This kept them busy, but he said he worked with highly trained and dedicated people. I would see this when I met with his crew on board their patrol boat.

Turning to Al, he said, "Good luck, Al, with your test." He petted her again on the head and said, "We have great confidence in you."

Donatella smiled tightly, hoping Al would emerge from this test as a certified canine lifeguard.

Donatella had worked with Al every day and saw that she was good-natured, curious, and attentive, and she had immediately showed a great aptitude to swim and rescue people. Donatella had faith in Al, but she could be stubborn and do what she wanted to do rather than obeying. Donatella had been consistent, calm, and firm with Al, but she didn't know how she would perform during the lifeguard test and that made her nervous. She hoped Al would not embarrass her.

21

Semper Paratus Backstroke

We all begin somewhere, and for Al this was her beginning. Whether she would succeed or fail was up to her.

Marco, the captain of the patrol boat, and a crewman gave us permission to come on board. He informed us that they were on patrol. They would be sailing through Genoa's harbor and along the coastline to make sure that boats and ships were operating safely and legally. That was their first priority. They had been ordered by the admiral to conduct the canine lifeguard rescue drill at a designated spot south of Genoa.

The crewman pushed the patrol boat off the dock and suddenly I felt like we were on another great adventure.

It was a feeling of freedom, of riding on the water. There was something magical about being able to float; it was unlike anything else in the world.

Yellow-legged gulls making laughing calls and mew gulls making high sharp squeaks circled overhead. Quickly the men got under way. Although this was Al's first time on board the Guardia Costiera's boat she looked relaxed, as if she had been doing this all her life.

Marco glanced at Al. He was not sure about having a dog on board. He had never worked with water rescue dogs. As Marco steered the boat through the harbor, past piers and docks, he and his crewman checked the area where the merchant vessels, cruise ships, and yachts were docked. Everything around us was in motion: workers were operating enormous cranes unloading cargo, trucks were picking up crates of food, tourists and fishermen were everywhere.

"It is such an honor to be out on the boat with you, and what you do is tremendously important," I said.

Marco nodded seriously and said that it helps to have more eyes on the water. He said that not everyone splashes their arms up and down to signal they are drowning. They may be silently drowning, a term coined by a man in the U.S. Coast Guard.

Marco explained that silent drowning happens when people's mouths are at or below the water's surface. They cannot shout for help. Their arms are struggling to tread water so they cannot wave for help. They are fighting for their lives.

Even those who are supervising people in the water may not recognize many of the signs of distress. The Guardia Costiera has learned to look for specific signs, including a swimmer with their head low in the water, their head tilted back, glassy eyes, or hair covering their face. The swimmer may be gasping or hyperventilating. They may be trying to swim but are not able to move forward.

I said that I had friends who were lifeguards, and one of their greatest challenges was to notice when someone suddenly slipped underwater. A child or an adult could be knee-deep in the water and suddenly the bottom drops and they go under in an instant. They may drown in only thirty seconds. That's why lifeguards constantly scan the water; but parents need to always be watching their children when they are near or in the water. And people need to watch one another. At the beach a wave can hit a child or an adult, knocking them instantly underwater, and if they can't swim, someone needs to have seen that happen and signal a lifeguard for help.

The colors of Genoa's signature skyline—terra cotta, orange, stone, gold, peach, and yellow—glowed in the morning light and reflected on peaceful sapphire-blue waters. The warmth exuded by the colors gave me the feeling that we were surrounded by a perpetual sunrise. The shape of the harbor created a natural amphitheater, and the sounds of cranes moving cargo, shouts of men, rumbles of engines, putter of small motors, clang of clips against masts, rush of water breaking against the boat bows, and the hum of conversation played like a symphony of the sea. I loved being there.

We sailed past ferries with people standing on deck. Some acknowledged the Guardia Costiera and waved. The men responded with a nod, but when people saw Al, they pointed at her, speaking excitedly in Italian and in other languages. They saw that the Newfoundland was wearing her red rescue harness, that she was on board a Guardia Costiera patrol boat, and they recognized her as a water rescue dog. They applauded and cheered her.

Al loved the attention and turned her head and watched for people passing on ships and boats. She looked intently through portholes and windows and made eye contact with passengers on deck.

When Marco glanced at Al, he smiled. He said his job was often intense and serious. He had to enforce the laws of navigation along the Italian coast and at sea. He made sure that the yachts, fishing boats, and merchant vessels were all being operated safely. Sometimes people became angry and unpredictable. There were times he had to rescue people in danger and put himself at risk. He was aware of all the boat traffic going in and out of the port of Genoa and was listening to the radio for updates from the Guardia Costiera base.

He noticed a yacht sailing near the harbor wall and told us to hold on.

Marco rapidly changed course and skillfully intercepted the yacht. He told us to move toward the stern, explaining that the yacht's captain was sailing in a restricted area that was only to be used by ferryboats. The yacht captain had created a dangerous situation. Ferryboats held specific courses and speeds, and a ship as large as a ferry could not stop quickly, so the ship's captain might not see a yacht and run it over.

The crewman asked the yacht's captain for his papers to make sure he was licensed. He explained the situation and issued a citation. The yacht captain disagreed and angrily signed the ticket, but just before he turned away, he noticed Al and asked if she was one of the canine lifeguards. Marco said yes, and the man's anger dissipated and he almost smiled.

When we pulled away from the yacht, Donatella told Marco that one of her friends was a ferryboat captain. He was an instructor at the school and had a canine lifeguard, a Newfoundland that trained at the school and with the Guardia. He also had a Labrador who was a working dog. The Lab's job was to sniff cargo and search for drugs and stowaways, and he did his job well. Marco agreed that in some situations, dogs were helpful to have on board but he was still skeptical of Al.

Al and Donatella returned to the bow of the boat and

the crew continued patrolling south along the Italian Riviera, through the Ligurian Sea's light sapphire-blue waters. We were sailing about eight hundred meters offshore so the crew could see the boats operating in the coves and along the shoreline and farther out to sea.

The ride in the large patrol boat was smooth, and the captain and crewman kept us moving at an efficient rate of eight to ten knots. The ocean was clear with visibility of three to four meters and so calm it mirrored a vibrant blue sky. We slid past pastel-colored hotels and buildings built on cliffs and rock slabs.

Donatella was agitated and biting her lip. Her nervousness was increasing. She was waiting to take on one of her life's most important challenges.

Sitting near the bow she kept looking at the water and glancing apprehensively at Al. She was focused and quiet. Bob said a few words to her in a steady voice. I think he was trying to reassure her that everything was going to be okay. She responded in clipped sentences.

Al was sitting regally beside her. Maybe Donatella had forgotten Al's pedigree. Maybe she didn't realize Al had greatness within her. Through Al's veins flowed the DNA of brave dogs that sailed across the stormy Atlantic with John Cabot, the great Italian and English adventurer who explored Labrador and the coast of North America. In Al's DNA were genes from dogs that dragged ashore bulging nets filled with cod in the frigid waters near the

Grand Banks for Spanish, French, and Portuguese fishermen. Pumping through Al's heart were the same traits of calmness, courage, and strength that Lord Byron admired in Boatswain, his beloved Newfoundland. In Al's spirit were the same characteristics as Seaman, the courageous Newfoundland that protected Lewis and Clark and their Corps of Discovery. Al had all of these qualities and all of this potential.

The wind was puffing up Al's long brown coat and blowing the fur away from her face. She was watching the water, turning, studying the shore. Al's eyes shone with intensity.

We passed many small coves and sandy beaches where people were swimming, floating on inflatable rafts, diving off ski boats and small wooden boats, and having fun in the water. Marco continued driving the boat south and the coastline became rockier. Elegant hotels built on cement pilings hugged cliff walls. We sailed through the waters off Camogli—the Gulf of Paradise. Pastel-painted baroque buildings wrapped around the shoreline and were terraced above a small harbor where traditional small white and blue-and-white and green wooden fishing boats were moored. The water offshore was crystalline blue and green.

Beyond the protection of the cove the wind was steadily increasing and the water was becoming choppy. Donatella spoke with Marco and they agreed that they could not wait any longer. They planned to go farther down the coast, but they did not have time. If they waited, the wind would be too strong to do the test.

Donatella suggested that they find a beach where a lot of people were in the water. The crowd would make it more difficult for Al to locate a person in distress, more like a real-life situation. And more challenging.

Al had been working with instructors at the school and had been able to tell when one of the members of the school was in trouble and she had been able to rescue them.

This test was different and it was extremely important. This would be the first time Al would be required to rescue a stranger.

It made sense that Donatella was nervous. The Guardia Costiera were watching her. They were complete professionals. If Al failed it would reflect on Donatella as an instructor and vice president of the school. It would be a disaster.

When the patrol boat reached the next swimming beach Donatella would swim to shore and ask a volunteer to be a victim. The volunteer would swim out one hundred meters and lift his or her arms to signal that he or she was in distress. Al would have to recognize the situation on her own. She would have to jump into the water and swim to the victim.

Al needed to pass. If she failed, it would be many more

months of training, maybe even a year, before the Guardia Costiera would invite her to attempt the test again.

Soon the patrol boat reached a sandy beach between Camogli and Portofino. Donatella spoke quickly to Bob. Handing him Al's leash, she suddenly was eager to see how Al would perform. Two years of hard work and intense training came down to this day.

Donatella took off her windbreaker, slipped off her shoes and pants, and waited for Marco to get closer to the shore. She jumped into the water and swam to the beach. Al whined and yanked on the leash and tried to follow her, but Bob restrained her, insisting that she sit. She continued to whine.

Donatella disappeared into the crowd on the beach. After a few minutes she found a woman who could easily swim two hundred meters who volunteered to be the victim. Donatella swam back to the boat and climbed on board. She played with Al to distract her while the woman swam out into the sea.

The woman started lifting her arms and dropping them on the water.

Al immediately saw her and started barking loudly. She was relentless, signaling to Donatella that someone needed to be rescued. Al jumped in the water followed by Donatella. They sprinted three hundred meters to the victim. Al circled around the distressed swimmer, presented the harness so she could grab the handle. Al waited until the woman grabbed the handle and held on. Then Al swam toward shore, pulling the woman with Donatella beside her.

Donatella asked the woman to let go of the handle. Al immediately felt the resistance change. She rapidly circled the woman and again presented the handle.

Al was performing just as she had been trained.

The volunteer held on and Al pulled both her and Donatella to the beach. When Al was knee-deep in the water, she did exactly what Mas had taught her. She waited for the woman to stand and escorted her all the way up onto the sand.

People on the beach stood up and applauded Al. Donatella was thrilled. After all the effort, Al had passed the test. She had earned her water rescue dog certification. People were gathering around them, saying Al's name, petting her, hugging her, and giving her a hero's welcome. Al had done it.

When Donatella and Al returned to the patrol boat Donatella was laughing and smiling for the first time that day. She hugged and kissed Al. Bob was thrilled for her. Marco, his crewman, and I were amazed. Al had done everything perfectly. She was always prepared—*Semper paratus*—and she was never afraid.

Marco and his crewman congratulated Al and Donatella, who was relieved. Finally, Al had reached the goal Donatella always hoped she would achieve. While being disappointed at times, she'd never given up on Al.

Donatella asked if it would be okay for me to get in the

water. She knew I was eager to cool off and to experience the salt water off Genoa for the first time. Marco said the admiral had already given his permission for me to do that.

Donatella thought it would be good to give Al another opportunity to rescue someone she barely knew. She asked if I minded posing as a victim. I was thrilled at the chance to participate.

When Marco gave me clearance, I jumped into the water and started swimming backstroke. I was planning to swim one hundred meters from the boat and then lift my arms to signal to Al that I needed help.

I took three strokes and Al started barking. I continued swimming backstroke. She would not stop barking. Donatella gave her permission to jump into the water. She jumped in and swam in a circle around me.

Donatella yelled at me to stop and dove in and raced to me.

"It's your backstroke!" she exclaimed.

"What?" I asked.

"Your backstroke. Al sees you. You are lifting your arms."

She suddenly realized something and she was so excited. "Now I know," she said. "Al saw you lifting your arms when you were doing backstroke. Yesterday she saw that too. Al thought you were giving her a distress signal!" she said, and her eyes opened wider.

"The dragonfly. It was lifting its wings. The ducks. They were lifting their wings. Al saw things no other dog saw. She is a different dog. These were signals to her. They were distress signals. That's why she chased them. That's what she was trained to do. She wanted to rescue them," she said.

"Al wanted to rescue them all," she repeated, and she realized that Al was an exceptional dog.

Al saw her joy. She felt it. She smelled it. Donatella had always had a place in Al's heart. Now Al had finally found a place in hers.

I swam to the Guardia Costiera.

Al swam to Donatella, choosing her above all else.

"*Brava*, Al, *brava*," Donatella said with elation.

A hot breeze stirred the azure-blue waters as we rode through one-meter waves back to Genoa, past the lighthouse and into the sheltered harbor. Marco pulled the boat along the dock and shook Donatella's hand again. He congratulated her. He petted Al and told her she was a great dog. He told Donatella he looked forward to working together with them again soon.

Mario radioed the base commander to let him know that the mission had been completed, that it had been successful, and he was ready to return to base.

Admiral Angrisano invited us to have a celebratory lunch at the base with Marco and more of his crew. The admiral planned to drop by when we were finished.

The good news spread fast. When we walked through the security gate on base, men and women in Guardia Costiera uniforms came over to congratulate Donatella and Al. They appreciated the training Donatella and Al had done, the skill the Newfoundland had developed, and the dedication required to have passed the test.

We ate a lunch of spaghetti with Bolognese sauce and Donatella gave Al some special treats she had carried with her in case she passed the test.

Somehow Al knew the treats were for a job well done. Eating them quickly, she sat beside Donatella, watching her with her golden eyes and hoping for more.

Admiral Angrisano arrived and shook Donatella's hand to congratulate her and rubbed the Newfoundland behind the ears and congratulated her for reaching the rank of a water rescue dog with the Guardia Costiera. Elated, Al thumped her tail against the floor.

Accompanying the admiral was the wife of a ship captain. The woman turned to Donatella and said that she and her husband had a two-year-old spinone Italiano. I asked Donatella what that was and she said the spinone was an ancient dog bred for hunting.

The woman's dog was waiting for her in the car. She asked if we would like to see it.

We walked outside with her and she opened the passenger-side door and grabbed her dog's leash. The dog leaped out, wagging his tail.

The spinone was a medium-sized dog, muscular and strong, with endurance. His owner said he was loyal, friendly, alert, and sweet—good with people and other dogs—and he needed a lot of exercise. The spinone came to me. He had sweet, expressive eyes, framed by shaggy eyebrows and a tufted moustache. His beard and coat were a beautiful orange roan—like the splatter marks in a Jackson Pollock painting. The dog let me pet him. His coat was short, close-lying, and wiry. Al moved between the spinone and me to make sure she got her share of affection.

The captain's wife asked Donatella if her dog could attend the water rescue school. Donatella said it was possible. Spinones have webbed paws and are good swimmers.

The woman said her dog was a good swimmer, and she wanted to train him to be a lifeguard dog just like Al.

22

Victory Lap Gelato

We left the Guardia Costiera building and walked back toward Donatella's car.

Somehow people in Genoa knew that something special had happened to Al. Maybe it was the way she was sauntering beside Donatella with her head and tail held high. Maybe they felt her exuberant energy and saw the light of happiness shining in her golden eyes. Maybe they saw the way Donatella was confidently walking beside her. Whatever it was, people throughout the city were stopping Donatella and Al.

When one man asked if Al was a water rescue dog, Donatella said proudly, *"Sì, lo è"*—"Yes, she is." It was something she'd wanted to say for most of Al's life, and now she had achieved that status. But more than that, she realized that Al was a different dog, different from all others she had ever raised or known. She was far more sensitive than Donatella ever realized and noticed things no other dog saw. Others had considered Al a failure, but now Donatella knew they'd been wrong. She was different and she was special. And Donatella realized that she had succeeded too. A deep sense of happiness radiated through her body. She glowed with pride. And it seemed to be growing as she began to realize how far they had come. It had taken a lot of courage to put herself out there with Al and know that they would be criticized. But they had moved beyond that and now there were new things to dream about and do. But for right now, it was time to celebrate their success.

A young girl wearing a bright cotton dress and eating strawberry gelato waved at Al with her free hand. Her mom asked if it was okay if her daughter petted the Terranova hero dog.

Donatella told Al to sit and she immediately obeyed. She towered above the little girl and looked longingly at her ice cream cone.

The little girl's mother warned her to hold her gelato aside so Al would not take a bite. The Newfoundland managed to swivel around her and lapped the gelato off her face. She wagged her tail quickly when the little girl burst into laughter. Her mother let Al lick her again. The girl finished the gelato on top and shared the cone on the bottom with the dog.

We continued walking toward the Guardia Costiera, and Al's head turned when a door opened and she smelled the special Genoa dish of pesto made of crushed garlic, basil, olive oil, pine nuts, all with Parmesan cheese. The chef stepped out of his door to applaud Al the water rescue dog. She was delighted with the attention. She loved to be loved. And Donatella loved seeing her being praised.

The old woman whom Al had met earlier that morning said she knew Al was a real champion and had proven it. "*Brava,* Al!" she exclaimed and hugged her tightly.

Donatella was still processing what had happened during the day. Her throat tightened and she sounded choked up with emotion.

"I've gone on patrols with the Guardia Costiera at least twenty times. Today was the first time the crew called me by my name. Today was the first time they recognized me. Today was the day Al became a new member of the Guardia Costiera water rescue dog team." Her eyes filled with happy tears.

It had taken so much time, so much effort, and so much understanding to reach what had seemed like an unattainable goal. But they never gave up. She never gave up on Al and Al never gave up on her. They were a winning team.

Al's eyes seemed to glow with love. She licked Donatella across her face.

"Al, sei un campione"—"Al, you are a champion," she said and hugged her tightly. Al understood her and looked into her eyes, thumped her tail hard against Donatella's leg, and leaned affectionately against her.

She snuggled Al and smiled. They had won.

Soon they would begin training to do water rescues from helicopters. There was still so much to do.

Afterword

When I last saw Al, she was two years old. She is now eleven and living a great life with Donatella. Al earned her official water rescue dog certification from the Scuola Italiana Cani Salvataggio (SICS), the Italian School of Rescue Dogs.

Al and Donatella are patrolling the beaches in the Liguria region and on Lombardy's lakes in northern Italy. They are sailing with the Guardia Costiera naval units, performing rescue exercises, patrolling Italian waters, and helping the Guardia Costiera make them safer. Al loves training and lifeguarding with them. She is eager and excited to perform tasks with the Guardia and they love having her on board. Al also loves visiting children in hospitals in Milan. She is so gentle with them.

Al earned her rescue dog wings. She is performing helicopter rescue exercises with the search and rescue groups of the Italian Air Force, the Guardia di Finanza, and Civil Protection. Al has always loved to fly. Donatella said that when she was three months old, she arrived from Brussels and was with Donatella and Ferruccio when she saw her first helicopter. Her first flight in one was when she was five months old and she was calm, serene, and curious.

They flew over green meadows filled with wildflowers and did many maneuvers with the helicopter door wide open. Al sat there enjoying the wind in her face and the fantastic view. Since her first flight she has had a passion for helicopters. For her the helicopter cabin is like a home. Donatella shares her passion. When they see a helicopter flying overhead, they both track it and hope it will land and carry them into the sky so they can watch over the people below.

Al also earned her SICS instructor dog certification. She has been coaching other dogs on land, on the water, and in the sky to become lifeguard dogs. She is often requested to accompany other dogs on their first helicopter flight to teach them how to be calm and show them that there is nothing to be afraid of. Al has helped train hundreds of dogs.

Al has never rescued anyone in the water because the primary role of Al and Donatella and the Guardia Costiera is safety and prevention. If they see someone getting into trouble in or on the water, they advise them what to do, and people listen, especially when they see Al.

Through the years, Donatella and Al's bond has become unbreakable. They have been together twenty-four hours a day for the past eleven years. Al will always ask Donatella with a look for permission to do something or for help. She is always by Donatella's side and they are always checking on each other. If Donatella walks toward the water, Al is right behind her, ready to go.

Donatella has been teaching dogs at the SICS for twenty-eight years. She loves it as much today as when she started. She has taught more than four hundred dogs and owners. Each dog is interesting in his or her own way and each taught Donatella something. One of her most profound experiences was with Alyssha, the Newfoundland she had before Al who taught Donatella what harmony means—the beauty of swimming together, moving side by side, and thinking in unison.

And Al has taught Donatella the most difficult thing to teach—faith. Teaching students not to be afraid that their dog would leave them alone in the middle of the sea, and that when the owners stop fearing failure and trust their dogs the miracle happens. Convincing people to trust their dogs is a long process of growth, with ups and downs, but once trust is established everything becomes easier because they will be together in the water, on land, and in life.

There are about four hundred dog units throughout Italy, and about thirty rescues are carried out along the Italian coast during each swimming season. The school is celebrating thirty-one years, and Ferruccio has trained about one thousand dogs and owners in collaboration with his instructors.

When I'm home I swim in the open water with friends with fur and without. Lois Lane, a sweet golden retriever, is one of my favorite swimming partners. She did her first dog paddle with me. And now whenever I walk by her house, she looks out the window at me as if to ask, "Do you want to go for a swim?"

I also swim with my human friends Suzy, Kent, and Eileen and during our workouts we sometimes swim with Sparky, a black shepherd mix; Atlas, a tiny but mighty goldendoodle; Lexie, a goldendoodle; and Tiller, a sweet chocolate Labrador. We have been hoping to swim with Bob, a black Labrador; Jill, a chocolate Labrador; and Charlie Brown, a boxer mix. We've been trying to convince Beau, a massive English bullmastiff, and Finn, a giant Irish wolfhound, to swim, but they stop when the water gets up to their chests. I'm hoping that by next summer the neighborhood dogs, their owners, and I will be able to get them to join us. There is something so joyful about swimming with dogs, feeling their exuberance, and knowing that they are having as much fun as we are, if not more.

Perhaps one day you will have the chance to swim in Italy and you will look up and see a helicopter flying by with Donatella and Al watching over you.

Acknowledgments

I am especially thankful to Victoria Wilson, my editor at Knopf, who knew exactly how to guide me and help me tell the best story about Al.

Thank you, Martha Kaplan, my agent, who loves dogs as much as I do and was excited about this book from the moment she read the story. Andy Hughes and Kathy Hourigan, thank you for your steadfast support. I appreciate working with the Knopf team, especially Marc Jaffee, for all the work that he has done on preparing my manuscript for publication.

Many thanks to Gabriella Miotto, who translated my initial inquiries. Thank you, Suzy Sullivan, for your support and for putting me in touch with Linda Pasqualino, who provided invaluable assistance by translating all of my interviews and interviewee responses.

Donatella Pasquale and Ferruccio Pilenga, thank you so much for bringing me into your community of people and dogs and for showing me how you watch over people, make sure they are safe, and how you care for one another.

What you have done in Italy is a positive example for people around the world. You are a very special group.

Thank you to the American embassy in Italy for their enthusiasm and for helping me contact the Italian Coast Guard (Guardia Costiera) and the Italian School of Rescue Dogs (Scuola Italiana Cani Salvataggio) to learn Al's story.

PHOTO CREDITS

Page 2, top: Ferruccio Pilenga

Page 2, middle: Simone Galbiati

Page 2, bottom: Bettina Salmelin

Page 3, top: Simone Galbiati

Page 3, middle: Ferruccio Pilenga

Page 3, bottom: Ferruccio Pilenga

Page 4, top: SICS

Page 4, middle: SICS

Page 4, bottom: Oreste di Chiara

Page 5, top: Simone Galbiati

Page 5, middle: Donatella Pasquale

Page 5, bottom: Simone Galbiati

Page 6, top: SICS

Page 6, middle: Oreste di Chiara

Page 6, bottom: Donatella Pasquale

Page 7, top: Simone Galbiati

Page 7, bottom: SICS

Page 8, top: Danila Bombelli

Page 8, bottom: Simone Galbiati

A NOTE ON THE TYPE

This book was set in Adobe Garamond. Designed for the
Adobe Corporation by Robert Slimbach, the fonts are based
on types first cut by Claude Garamond (c. 1480–1561). Garamond was a pupil of Geoffroy Tory and is believed to have
followed the Venetian models, although he introduced a
number of important differences, and it is to him that we
owe the letter we now know as "old style." He gave to his
letters a certain elegance and feeling of movement that won
their creator an immediate reputation and the patronage of
Francis I of France.

Composed by North Market Street Graphics, Lancaster, Pennsylvania

Printed and bound by Berryville Graphics, Berryville, Virginia

Designed by Maggie Hinders